LOOKING FOR DON

For Our Friend
Andrea
With Love and
Thanks.

[signature]

2/28/12

LOOKING FOR DON

A MEDITATION
BY DAI SIL KIM-GIBSON

FOREST WOODS MEDIA PRODUCTIONS

FIRST EDITION. FIRST PRINTING

Looking for Don: A Meditation

Copyright © 2012 Dai Sil Kim-Gibson

Published by Forest Woods Media Productions

Cover photo by Dai Sil Kim-Gibson; author's photo by Christopher Li
Book design by Janice Olson
Printed by Lightning Source

Library of Congress Control Number: 978-0-938572-56-5
International Standard Book Number: 2011943859

For our friends

FOREWORD

D onald Gibson and Dai Sil Kim-Gibson were a great love story. "Don & Dai Sil" was one name to everyone who knew them.

Don was a senior executive, ending as acting Chair at the National Endowment for the Humanities under President Clinton. Dai Sil met Don at NEH when she worked as senior program officer at Media Program. They had heightened intellectual lives and what one noticed first is that each one was the other's reason to care about the world. They both had the same social concerns—injustice, inequality and human rights violations. In their private lives they were a fusion of surprise, humor, passion, furious debate and boisterous happiness.

How do we explain a young woman born in North Korea and a farm boy born on an Iowa farm meeting and marrying, each for the first time, at age 41, and then spending 30 years in mutual amazement at their similarities? How could these antithetical rhythms come together? How do we explain the contradictions of language and character that blended into a life-long relationship?

Dai Sil takes us by the hand through her last days with Don. She has the stunning ability to say what she means with courage and style. We readers have the privilege of sharing the feelings that let light through: dreams, poems, thought fragments, memory and daily events. This is high risk writing. Opening the heart to see what falls out is living fully. Doing it in public is living dangerously.

Life is not linear, nor are these personal accounts. Dai Sil holds out her ideas and experiences as they occur to her. This is the artist's way. The secret is to make it work for the reader. And it does, because of intelligence, talent and experience.

Dai Sil has summoned the spirit and energy to record her days with Don, and, after that, her conversations with the dead, through the discipline of daily writing. We can see the fundamental struggle to speak when grief knows so few words in the theater of language. Yet she speaks.

It would be unforgivable for a woman to love so deeply and not share it. She fills a void in us we did not know existed. This is an intimate look at the transformation of sorrow and grief's rugged beauty.

Ecclesiastes 3:1 "For everything there is a season, and a time for every matter under Heaven."

~ Grace Cavalieri
Producer, "The Poet and the Poem from the Library of Congress"

Don & Dai Sil

Dai Sil

"Dai Sil, wake up. It is a little after 5. Time to study."

My eyes closed, I plead, "Grandma, please let me sleep for five more minutes." As soon as I became a sixth grader, I had been getting up at 5 in the morning to study for the entrance examination to my chosen middle school, Ewha. My grandmother was an alarm clock. "Five more minutes, please" became a ritual. "Okay. I am going to sit right here with you and wake you up in ten minutes," says my grandma.

Our helpers (a cook and a babysitter) would put a large amount of washed rice in a big iron pot and cook. When the rice boiled, and simmered with the wood turning into ashes, they would open the pot and find rice cooked to perfection. After the rice was dished out into bowls for each of us, at the bottom lay my treat—rice stuck, turning into crisp gold, flat cake.

There were two ways of eating slightly burned rice, stuck at the bottom: to pour water into the pot and leave it to turn into a soft rice in water. The natural flavor from the rice became tasty, soothing soup. Much of the time, this was consumed by the helpers.

The second, the superior way, was to get the stuck rice out, clustered together, as if a huge rice cake. It took some skill to get it out with a steel tool. Our helpers could do it but the best among all of us was my grandmother. She could get the whole thing out with minimum damage. She would put that flat rice cake on a plate, sprinkle on some brown sugar and bring it to me.

That grandmother with a rice cake on a plate gave me invisible nourishment all through my life.

Don

My schooling took place in the same school for twelve grades. And school work was matched by farm work. My duties started as far back as pre-school days, but my parents waited until I turned 10 to assign me serious farm work. At that point, my father hauled a tractor and taught me to drive it. The task was harrowing a recently plowed field, to level it, root up weeds, and to break up clods, etc.

Soon I was driving the battered International pickup as well as the tractor. Farm boys were allowed, if only unofficially, to drive trucks under-aged and unlicensed, as long as they stuck to rural roads.

Of all the chores, the hardest and least loved was getting up early in the morning. No matter what the season, I would get up at 5 am. First I milked the cows, then separated cream and milk. My livestock care included not only cows, but also pigs and beef cattle, not to mention the beheading and plucking of chickens. And then there were seasonal chores, like earmarking piglets, or castrating slightly older pigs.

There was nothing romantic about my morning chores. Every time Dai Sil romanticized the farm life, I asked if she ever had to get up on a below zero winter morning to milk the cows.

The hard work, however, did not go unrewarded. My mother would cook me five eggs-over easy and thick strips of crispy bacon. I devoured them with homemade bread smothered with butter and jam. Sometimes she would make pancakes from scratch. During the school year, I would then change my clothes. By the time I waited for the school bus on a farm road, I felt happy, fresh air in my lungs.

Iowa corn field

Autumn

"All living is meeting. Feelings dwell in man,
but man dwells in his love."

Martin Buber

Autumn

From the star strewn sky
Comes a tale of love
Told from a great distance
Riding the wind
Through the shadows and darkness.
~ *dskg*

I've never thought that my husband, Don, would actually die. I had never thought about life without him ever since I found him. Everyone else, including me, will and can die, but not my Don.

Even before I found him, I had loved him in anticipation of finding him and now after he is gone, in my memories, he is more vivid than anything alive.

Don was born on a hot August day on an Iowa farm in 1938, while I became a month and two days old in a far away town in northern Korea. Later when we were wed, it gave him great pleasure to tell everyone that he married an older woman. Older or younger, Don and I were two tigers, both born in the year of tiger, never to be separated.

Don was a happy child, a loner but a cheerful and bright boy, making the best out of life with his very own limited re-sources. After he was gone, I came across his writings about his favorite place, the attic—hide away place where he spent hours and hours, reading and imagining things. One day as he read a Superman comic, lying on his belly, he came across a line about the year 2000. "Year 2000! Gosh, I would be 64 years old then. Yuck! How can anyone be as old as 64!" (Don told the story this way, but he actually turned 62 in 2000).

That little boy grew not only as old as 62 but lived to be 70, and became a bright, shiny star for me for more than 29 years until January 18, 2009.

ON OCTOBER 25, 2009, I WAS IN BOSTON for two days to receive a distinguished alumni award from my *alma mater*, Boston University. I wasn't keen about going but when they said I would stay at the Hyatt Hotel next to the university, my mind was made up. Yes.

For our honeymoon in 1979, Don and I stayed in a lovely home that belonged to parents of Richard Cohen, Don's best friend, in Wellfleet, Cape Cod. If those five days on Cape Cod were memorable, the few days that followed at the Hyatt Hotel in Cambridge were poignant and lovely.

I entered Room 520 at the Hyatt Hotel. Just as I did with Don in 1979, I could see Boston University straight across from the window of my room.

In that room now, in 2010, I see Don's bear hugs and smiles that had a thousand shapes and colors. Don's youthful face with unbridled energy appeared in my mind, but soon his old face— thinner and smaller—overshadowed it, the face that knew suffering. His face looked beautiful to me even in ICU. "You look

Don in our neighborhood, 2007

good, Don. Your face is beautiful enough for you to hit on some nurses," I would say. "Oh, sure, sure," he said with a grin.

After the Honors event, coming back home, I had a couple of hours to kill. I wandered by the Copley Square Hotel which

I had passed so many times in the sixties as a graduate student when I was too poor to enter. The last time Don and I were in Boston together, I suggested, "Let's come back sometime and stay at Copley Square just for fun," but we never did. So I walked into its opulent bar and ordered a glass of merlot in Don's honor. It was a good thing that I didn't look at the bill until I was ready to leave. The most expensive glass of merlot I've ever had, but every cent I spent on that wine was worth the memory.

I read a book by Amos Oz, *Rhyming Life and Death.* Speaking of a man and woman relationship, he writes, "If there is no electricity there, how on earth can they start to make a relationship? But if there is electricity then they end up getting burnt. And that's the reason why, Ricky (a character) thinks, one way or another love affairs always end in despair."

Ours was never a love affair. Ours was a life of love where our souls and minds met, destined to last in life and in death. We didn't need an electrical cord between us to be tied together.

Today I am reading a small book by Henri Nouwen, *Life of the Beloved.* Father Nouwen writes that the two major means to unite two people and make them one are eating together and having sex. During the early years of our marriage, Don devoured my food and made love, not with refined skills but with passion. But with Crohn's disease, his appetite became smaller and smaller and his energy less and less. Yet Don and I were one.

For sure, Don and I were one but it did not mean that we merged, and surrendered our individuality in our unity. We knew the meaning of dependence and independence which strengthened each other.

As Rainer Maria Rilke writes in *Letters to a Young Poet,* Don and I knew that "a solitude is a heightened and deepened kind of aloneness for the person who loves," and that "ultimately, and precisely in the deepest and most important matters, we are unspeakably alone." We both sought for vast inner solitude. We lived in the same space but we spent hours alone to walk inside ourselves. And we were in peace that we each did this.

After we got married, the kitchen table became our attic. If a bed was a usual place for a couple to merge, for us it was our kitchen table, laughter ringing out, ideas flying from one mouth to another, accompanied by the noise of chewing food, with a glass of wine, often Don's red and mine white.

Until our house fire in 2001, our kitchen table was the wooden one I had bought at This End Up. That table was also our playground, no, not making love, but playing countless yahtzee games. I still have a piece of paper where Don wrote down the scores of the game in which I made 209 points, glued on our refrigerator door. Don still owes me $80.

Alone at the kitchen table now, I hold a glass of wine, Don's face vivid in my mind's eye across the table and with fantastic glow of the setting sun outside of our living room window. As the wine warms my body, I remember all those nights when Don said at the top of his lungs, "I love you!" which is shouted in his office/study loud enough for me to hear in our master bedroom with the door closed.

I remember fragments of my dream last night.

> *I see Don climbing Mount Kumgang, widely known as Diamond Mountain. The magnificent mountain about which Koreans say, "One cannot die before one sees Mt. Kumgang."*
>
> *I can't see his face but back or front, I would know him anywhere. Trailing far behind, I plead, "Don, wait for me!" He does not wander around. He does not look back. He continues to climb, straightforward, his steps accelerated.*
>
> *High up on a rocky pinnacle piercing the sky, he stands and turns around. The sun illuminates his face. It is my Don.*

> *Sweat saturates me as I look up. In silence, I hear his giddy*
> *laughter. Tears fill my eyes. "Don, please do not vanish."*
> *"Come meet me at the sidewalk café where I stole the look of*
> *your hairy arm."*

I woke up as these words were carried to Don on a pinnacle
of Mt. Kumgang by the wind through my window.

JANUARY 6, 2009 THEY DID A SECOND ENDOSCOPY to find the
source of his internal bleeding. My cell phone rang. It was Mark,
Don's nurse practitioner for that day. He told me to come and
sit with Don. "He asked for you." Not yet the time when visitors
were allowed in the ICU but Mark told me that I could come.

Entering quietly his room, I found him sleeping. As he
opened his eyes, his eyes glistened with tears and his voice
cracked. "Don, I am here with you. And I will be with you
always. Be strong. We're going back home together," I said. He
looked at me, more tears filled his eyes, but color returned to
his face. He didn't say anything but his face told me, "Yes, we
will go back home together."

Then he dozed off again. I sat still watching him sleep. After
a while, I heard him, "The only thing." A pause in eerie quiet-
ness of the ICU room. "The only thing I know: I love you and
that is the only thing that keeps me going." Quietly I put those
words for keeps in my chest.

I am reading *Essential Writings* by Thomas Merton and find
this:

> And what is love? When you love another person you
> simply forget yourself and think about the other person.
> You are not concerned with yourself. And if you love the

other person and know that it is mutual then you know the other person is thinking about you. So what happens in love is that each one forgets himself in order to live in and for the other.

Don and I met when we were both 40. We had plenty of relationships which we thought were "love" but they failed because we loved as a male and female. When Don and I met, we were ready to love each other as human beings.

I look inside myself to see where feelings first began. What forms Love? With Don, I am sure Love came from the comfort of a farm family in Iowa. Mine, from Korea, the land of morning calm, the land of my birth.

I AM TWELVE YEARS OLD. Six of us, children, were living in a small room of a farm house with a thatched roof, each day like eternity, waiting for the war to end and bring back the scattered family—my father and eldest brother who had to run away to save their lives, and my grandmother who was nursing back my second brother from a shrapnel wound during the bombing of our house, in a rented room somewhere in Seoul.

Our mother, a delicate, fragile, and beautiful mother. She cooked rice, the rice for which she had exchanged her silk materials. She put a large bowl of steaming rice in the middle of the round table where the children sat around. No small bowls to serve each. My siblings used their spoons with vigor and speed. I tried to slow down my eating, slower than my usual "slow" habit of eating, to be faithful to my own determination to cultivate inner beauty by being good. (I had committed a birth crime by being born "ugly," well, at least not beautiful enough to meet the standard of either side of the family, which prompted me to try to become beautiful inside.) I barely made two spoonfuls of rice when the large bowl became empty. It went on for several days.

One day at a meal, I found a separate bowl of rice in front of me. "This is for you, Dai Sil. You wouldn't be able to survive if you had to eat from the large bowl. Eat as slowly or as fast as you wish but it is your rice!"

That little bowl of rice made my body and soul flood with feelings that were as soft as the clouds on a clear Spring day, as warm as a battered blanket that covered me on a cold Winter night, as lovely as a dream in which I flew in silk shoes and colorful Korean costume, as delicious as a layered rice cake with turnip and red bean, as hopeful as a future floating in front of me, only to be caught by me.

What was in that bowl was not rice at all. It was love I've taken for granted. It was love from the woman who sheltered and raised me in her womb and brought me out to the world.

"Relationship" does not die even after the death of the loved one. My relationship with Don as a wife, best friend and soul mate did not die when his body disappeared. Not one bit.

How can it? I find what Don wrote on the second anniversary of our house fire, which turned the house and everything in it into ashes.

> *December 29, 2003, two years after the disaster. My health remains problematic but I am, hopefully, putting all that behind me. I have life, Dai Sil and hope.*

I was one of three that Don held onto after the disaster which nearly destroyed him. Life, Dai Sil and hope.

Don lists me between life and hope. I gave him a reason to live and hope. Death could not take away our relationship.

I found Don's writing about our wedding, describing it as one of the intense moments of his life, our wedding in the Muelder house (George W. Muelder, the retired dean of the School of

Theology, was my mentor who married us) in Newton Centre, Massachusetts.

I can still see Dai Sil coming down the stairs with Martha Muelder playing the piano and Walter waiting in the living room to perform the ceremony. I cried and barely had the wherewithal to say "I do" and place the ring on Dai Sil's finger.

I REMEMBER DON'S FINAL DAYS ON EARTH. Only a couple of days before he left me, he noticed that his wedding ring was missing. He was concerned where it was. "I have it," I told him. "Your nurse and I had to take it off. I wanted to put it back but couldn't because your fingers were so swollen. I'll keep it safe. See, I'm wearing it."

His face relaxed, even looked youthful.

I found a long write-up about rings in Don's computer.

I never liked diamonds, considering them wasteful, expensive and ostentatious. Thus, during our engagement, I asked Dai Sil if she wanted a diamond ring. She said no and I readily accepted her judgment. I wonder still if she meant that or was simply pleasing me. She has joked about it in the intervening years. [I wish I could tell Don again that I really meant it]. *We instead went to a jewelry store in Washington and purchased gold bands. After Crohn's reduced my weight significantly, including on my fingers, I managed to lose my ring at the time of my mother's death. We were in Arizona and Iowa and then back to Washington when, sitting at the kitchen table with Dai Sil, I glanced at my hand and noticed that I had no ring. I clutched my hand and felt awful. Dai Sil then had the ingenious idea of splitting her ring in two. We found another jeweler in D.C. This was in 1994, after the fall of the Soviet Union, and the jeweler's craftsman was Russian. He said it would be difficult but he could handle it. He did, magnificently. So now we both wear one half of Dai Sil's original ring.*

I now wear two rings on my wedding finger.

> Faces crimson with passion
> With magical friendship
> Will never be adrift,
> But lured together
> To fly through
> The wide expanse of sky.
>
> Despite alarming clouds
> Their hearts enchanted are
> Two hearts tied to one in gladness.
>
> ~ dskg

I miss talking with him. Laughing with him.

A story he once told me:

At the end of one school year, actually the night before report cards were to be handed out, I attended a delightful dinner party which lasted longer than I had anticipated. Around midnight, I drove to the school in order to finish grading and assign the grades. A bit too much in a hurry, I was stopped by a highway patrolman who, after a pleasant chat during which I was at my most charming, he gave me only a warning ticket and sent me on my way.

The following morning I handed out the report cards and was standing alone in my classroom when the same patrolman walked in, fully uniformed with his pistol at his side. I was confused but it soon became apparent that I had flunked his daughter.

I do not know if he didn't give me a ticket because he knew I was his daughter's teacher. I certainly didn't know he was the father. He probably knew.

I can still hear both of us laughing each time he told that story.

WE WENT TO YMCA TO GET SWIMMING LESSONS when we lived on the 17th Street, D.C. Don was a lousy swimmer and I was even worse, but he excelled in diving and I was even worse in diving than in swimming. The swimming instructor pointed me out as an example of what not to do. Every time I landed on my belly, Don cheered. He would say on the way home, "Dai Sil, what you did back there is belly flop!" and then laughed his head off. I was mad enough to want to kill him but how can you kill a guy with such hearty laughter?

I asked big, small and all questions, even the ones which I thought I already knew. I found Don's writing about one of those questions in his computer.

This morning at breakfast Dai Sil looked up from reading the newspaper and asked where the phrase, "Where's the beef?" came from. Amazingly, I knew the answer. In the 1984 campaign for the Democratic party nomination for President, Walter Mondale, the former Vice President, was the presumptive favorite but was challenged by Gary Hart. Mondale, attempting to cast his opponent as callow, when Hart used the repeated phrase of "new ideas" in the debate, yelled, "Where's the beef?" the commercial of the fast food chain, Wendy's. Dai Sil nodded and then said, "Well, in Korea that's what we asked when we were

> *served beef stew. 'Where's the beef?' There would be*
> *only one tiny piece, if that.'"*

MIAE (MY BEST FRIEND) HAD AN UNUSUAL EYE for detecting antiques. In the 1970s, Miae and Yongjin bought quite a few Korean antique chests. One day when I visited them in their Dobbs Ferry house, I noticed a beautiful antique chest which stood out from all other pieces. I admired it with my mouth wide open. Miae's response was immediate and flippant, "If you ever get married, it will be our wedding gift!" At that point, she had given up the idea of wedding bells for me.

Miae kept her word. I recall Don's face on the day Miae and Yongjin brought the chest to our Washington, D.C. home.

The first time I visited Don's apartment on Capitol Hill, my eyes were drawn to two black foot stools, clearly not store bought but I could not quite figure out what they were. "How unusual!" I said pointing to them. Don announced that he had crafted them during his graduate school days in 1965. He welded two tire rims together and a specially sawed round piece of plywood for the top. The rims were painted black. I was impressed.

When we married, one of the first things I did was to paint the top with cadmium yellow over black. A small addition to my farm boy husband's ingenious craft.

They were the most beautiful foot stools you ever saw. He still loved fixing things when we were married, happy to make me happy.

DON ENJOYED TEASING ME about my rough feelings towards Japan since I started making films on such horrendous topics as sex slavery *(Silence Broken: Korean Comfort Women)* and forced laborers *(A Forgotten People: the Sakhalin Koreans).* I find a file in Don's computer, "Dai Sil and Japan."

Dai Sil is always sympathetic and exceedingly generous to those in need. But, on May 26, 2003, she was walking in our neighborhood and was confronted by a homeless man who asked for some money. She reached in her pocket, pulled out a dollar bill and was about to hand it to him. He said, "God praise Japan." Dai Sil immediately withdrew the dollar and marched forward. I'm afraid he never understood.

At Mount Holyoke College, I co-taught a class (Religion and Political Systems) with a man from British Guyana who studied at Oxford as many upper class people from that country did. He spoke English with a perfect Oxford accent, but streams of cuss words often flew out of his mouth with elegance. I asked him to teach me. By the end of the semester, he declared that I surpassed him.

Later in my life, I enjoyed using them from time to time simply to see the shock on the faces of those "superior" white folks. Those words emerging out of a sweet mouth of an Asian woman, supposed to be "submissive" and "shy."

Don and I started using them for fun. We said them well and sometimes with feelings but they didn't mean anything to us. Once driving alone in the car for a couple hours, I felt terribly sleepy. In order to stay awake, I started translating all the obscene words into Korean. I could not say them aloud. There was no one but me in the car in a pitch dark night but still I could not say the same words I so often uttered. When I said them in English, they didn't mean anything, but spoken in Korean, they burned my face red with fear and shame. The words I was never to utter as a well brought-up kid.

One of the most frequently used words between us was "asshole," I often saying "arsehole," imitating stuffy Brits. When Don and I got irritated with each other, instead of raising our voices or fight, we said, "What an asshole you are" and grinned. That "arsehole" went away, and left me alone.

In relation to shit, the most endearing story is of the pony hidden under piles of shit. The story, known to many, became special to us by Don who relayed it to me with exaggerated flair. One Christmas, Don brought me a small, navy blue velvet box. "Open it. I hope you'll like it." Out came a dazzling, gold pony. I did not wear it often, fearful that I might lose it. I still have it. My gold pony.

———

EARLY ON IN OUR LIFE TOGETHER, I looked at myself in the mirror. "Don, do I have a fat face?"

Don exploded in laughter. "No, Dai Sil, you don't have a fat face. You have the most beautiful face on earth."

Laughing, Don added, "Ol' Fool, I love you more than I ever could express! You are everything to me. And you are beautiful."

Mr. Gibson declared Mrs. Gibson beautiful.

That Mr. Gibson is gone now.

I look at myself in the mirror. Today I decided to declare again my face "beautiful" since it is the face Don loved. I don't care what others think of my face. I know Don went away loving my face.

But my grief persists. It feels like quiet stream in the midst of thick forest, water passing through pebbles and stones like sad melodies.

I would be working. Then suddenly Don's absence grabs me and I am lost, my body and mind soaked by a melodic stream of sadness.

I am still struggling that he is dead and I am alive. How can he be dead and I am alive?

> *There are memories*
> *That will not fade*
> *Into a darkening night*
> *To be swept into a void.*
>
> *There are memories*
> *That the stain and bruise*
> *Left by Death*
> *Cannot erase.*
>
> *At the edge of the world,*
> *If the memories make one weak*
> *With remembering,*
> *The soul will heal and shelter,*
> *To conjure more memories.*
> *~ dskg*

LAST NIGHT, I WAS AT THIS FANCY TABLE, all dressed up in black and white, and suddenly I found myself crying. Sadness, that piercing sadness, invaded me in the middle of a tasteless filet mignon dinner and made me cry. Up at the podium, a woman, supposed to be the US ambassador to Korea, was uttering boring words—all of them sounding like "US/Korea relationship." And I kept crying, wiping tears with my napkin. If people thought I was moved by that stupid speech, let them. I just missed my Don. The last time I attended that dinner with Don, he was in his tuxedo and I made myself my own tuxedo with a black pants suit and a bow tie. We were the cutest couple. Why wasn't he there with me?

This afternoon, I went for a walk. Entering the lobby of our apartment, I practically collapsed on a lobby couch, exhausted. A big doorman Eli was there, the man who had turned into a kind friend to Don.

Suddenly I started to cry and Eli brought me a piece of paper towel. I wiped tears, got in the elevator and entered the apartment. I took one of a few remaining bell oranges, from Harry and David, sent by Young Sook Han. I've been eating one a day, enjoying every bit of its sweet juice. Those oranges are not something I am willing to give away but I took one and brought it to Eli for his compassion filled piece of paper towel and his kindness toward Don.

Night. After eating some food, I felt much better.

I found a mail from Maryann, a filmmaker friend with whom I had traveled to Korea to make short pieces on Korea during the 1988 Olympics. We both worked for Jon Alpert, a pioneering video maker. I found her after a couple decades, of all the places, on my television screen as I accidentally caught her receiving an Academy Award for *Chernobyl-heart,* a 30-minute documentary dealing with the nuclear power explosion in Ukraine. Her mail read, "It's the sweetest and sanest thing I've heard that you talk to Don. He must be out there somewhere listening." She went on. "Dai Sil, when you wrote 'I'm living on the power of my loneliness,' it hit me hard. How devastating that must be to lose your soul mate. That's why I don't know what to write, how can I say anything to the depth of that feeling. Words are too poor."

I AM CONSUMED BY ANGER. "How can he leave me? We were go-ing to grow old together!"

Soon I chase anger away, only feel sadness with "unbearable lightness of being." When that book, *The Unbearable Lightness of Being* by Milan Kundera, came out, I read and understood with my head. Now I feel it with my heart and soul. I go to my com-puter and search for more writings by Don. I am surprised to find a document, entitled "The Americans on the Isle of Arran." Trying to quiet down my pounding heart, I read on.

> *Isle of Arran*
>
> *My family on my father's side actually hailed to America from Ireland, not Scotland, but I've always considered Scotland the country of my ancestors. My father preferred to think of himself as Irish, not Scot-tish, but really he is Scotch-Irish. So am I. I was thrilled to go to Scotland for our vacation.*
>
> *We left D.C. for Glasgow on the 26th of August, 1994. From Glasgow, we took a ferry and arrived on August 27 onto the Isle of Arran. We took a bus from Braddick dock to reach hotel Kildoran where Dai Sil had booked us.*
>
> *The island is 19 miles long by 10 miles wide. Along the way, we passed a succession of velvety green hills— so many different shades of green as Dai Sil never failed to point out every Spring as the new growth sprouted on the trees. If there is such a thing as "pure" green, I surely thought these hills seen from the bus must exemplify it. But I didn't say so to her. Suddenly, the winding road opened up to an astounding view of the sea.*
>
> *The Deightons, the owner of the hotel, told us to make ourselves at home. That night, we sat in their liv-ing room by the fireplace and drank Laphroaig, single*

malt Scotch we had been introduced to by the mystery novels of Dick Francis. The hero in his books always drank it. A roaring fireplace at the end of August on the Isle of Arran with Dai Sil. At that moment, all I wanted was to stop the time and sit there forever. I sound like Dai Sil, but that's how it was.

The hotel owner's son gave us another tour of the island. He drove us along the island's interior, through a scenic mountain valley populated by streams, mountains, sheep and deer. Heather seemed to cover half of the mountains. Each time, the winding road curved, another spectacular view. It was exhilarating. He also took us along on his boat when he went to catch lobsters.

We stayed at the Kildoran for a week, and I was sad to leave our hotel Kildoran. Mr. Deighton handed me the "bill." It was a collection of hand-scribbled, stapled together fragments of paper where meals and drinks were itemized, plus our nightly room charge. I was utterly charmed to note that under "guests" name," it simply said "the Americans."

Shortly after we returned from Scotland, we had our 15th anniversary. I remember Don's card in which he wrote, "Dai Sil, I want you to know that without you, I am nothing. You are my meaning."

I SIT ALONE ON THE SECOND DAY OF THE SECOND MONTH of 2009. Don had been gone for almost two weeks. I decided to be brave—dressed, do laundry, pick up the apartment a little.

As I folded and stacked, there was not a single article of clothing that belonged to Don, not an undergarment, not a sock. The

Don on Cape Cod, 1979

only item that had anything to do with him was a placemat that held his dinner on the 2nd of January, the last dinner we had together before he was rushed to the hospital the very next morning.

I will not wash his things any more, will I? I will not press his shirts and pants on an ironing board in the apartment building's basement laundry room.

I remembered how I would put out carefully coordinated clothing for him to wear each day. I wanted my "shrunken old man" (one of my endearments for him as he fretted about old age and illness) to look nice and neat. I often said, "Don, you look good," once he was dressed for a little walk. "My wife dresses me!" he'd reply with a grin.

I wonder if Don knew that it warmed my heart to do his laundry. He was always so worried about my lifting the heavy baskets, especially after my surgery for stomach cancer in 2005.

I was not supposed to lift heavy things. But between the two of us, I still had more strength than he. It vexed him that I had to do "everything." He wanted to be able to do more things for me.

Tears gather in my eyes as I remember Don in the ICU. Even while he was dying, Don never failed to ask me if I had eaten. He was worried about my eating, which became a big concern after my stomach surgery.

More memories in the ICU come and I am lost in them. Out of the blue, he decided that he craved a hot fudge sundae. I asked him if he would choose that over Scotch neat. In the early days, that used to be his wish for his "death bed." He thought about it a little, smile returning to his eyes, and uttered a firm "yes."

At that moment, my only wish in life was to run out and bring him ice-cream covered with hot chocolate. But no food of any kind was allowed. "Don, when we are together again, let us have ice cream and Scotch neat in front of a flaming fire place."

> *On our palette are many colors.*
> *Can we pick one color on our palette*
> *and call it a truth?*
>
> *If not one color,*
> *Could it be each color*
> *Has its own shadow?*
>
> *What truth will lead us to the core of life?*
> *If we unleash them all at once,*
> *There will be a catastrophe of confusion.*
> *The cacophony can drown us*
> *Into a sea of panic and sadness.*
>
> *There is a floating straw in the sea.*
> *Grasp it. It is love.*
>
> ~ *dskg*

I went to Book Culture on 112 Street between Broadway and Amsterdam to have a break from obsessive thought of Don's passing. But instead of a repose, the book store took me back to the morning of January 9, 2009.

On that morning of January 9, I got up late, around 8, after a very rough night. I poured lots of milk into cold coffee, warmed it in the microwave and drank it with a piece of corn bread I had brought from my lunch the previous day. Then I decided to hop on the M4 bus and go to Book Culture to buy Don some books. Don had run out of light books.

That morning, the bus was a bit faster than usual, and I was off at 112 and Broadway with plenty of time to spare for stopping at St. John the Divine. I went to the Cathedral, lit a candle and concentrated all my being in prayer, asking God's miraculous hand yet one more time so that I could bring Don back home. My heart was filled with hope.

Then I went to the book store, and bought three books. I thought they could be too serious. So I picked up a collection of Agatha Christie's short stories from a street vendor for $5. I walked to 116 Street subway station and hopped on train #1. When I arrived at ICU, eager to see Don, it was noon, the time they would allow the visitors. I went in with my head down and in tip toe and stood in front of his room eager to see his face.

I wanted to see his face light up at the sight of me, as sick as he was.

Even from the door, I could see that his face was pale, and his lips parched. A nurse told me that he was suffering from an excruciating headache, a new symptom. I put on the yellow gown in a hurry and stood by him. I held his icy hands, and legs.

I was frantic that they help with his headache. I begged the nurses to help him. They told me in a matter of fact tone that the headache was mostly caused by the lack of blood and that they ordered more blood to transfuse in his body "Well, where is the blood?" I screamed.

The agony and pain I felt then was beyond any words. If I was in that much agony, how much more could be his? It was driving me insane, and terror of losing him squeezed me tight.

Finally, I saw his nurse with a bag of blood in her hand. Instead of hurrying into his room, she was chit-chatting with someone in front of Don's cubicle. I could not believe it. She had a bag of blood that could help my Don and she was visiting with a friend! I yelled at her, and she became defensive. "I went myself to get it and I am doing my best. . ." I said nothing but concentrated on staring at her. No more words of defense. She quietly put the blood bag up to drip in his body.

It was only in the evening that the color was back on his face and he seemed to be resting in relative comfort. Then, I heard him. "Well, my headache is almost gone." Oh, God, his headache is gone! A moment of pure joy for me.

Back home alone, I called Don on his cell phone. The use of cell phone was forbidden in his room. So Don had fixed his phone just to vibrate. That night as soon as I entered the apartment, I called him. At the second ring, I heard his voice. "I love you," I said, "and I promise that I will bring you home with me soon." He was quiet but I could feel the vibration of his heart full of hope.

Today, I went for a walk. These days instead of going to Fort Tryon Park, I go to Castle Village Garden, near my apartment, because that's where we had Don's Memorial. As I was entering the Garden, I saw purple irises in full bloom. Suddenly I saw Don in his powder blue suit (which he had claimed to be his best suit) with a bunch of purple irises. He came with those flowers to my Arlington apartment in 1979. They were the most beautiful flowers but his best suit dismayed me a little.

At the end of the evening, he confessed that he had stolen those flowers; he picked them up in the front yard of his rented apartment on East Capitol Street. We were both drenched in giddy and happy laughter.

Now looking at the purple irises in Castle Village Garden, I remembered the time I finally threw the blue suit away after we were married. It made him look like an awkward kid from a farm, dressed up for Sunday school.

How did it happen that I didn't give our last kiss that he requested?

Three days before his final departure, as I was leaving the ICU, Don asked me to "kuss" him (once I said kuss for kiss by mistake. So from then on, it was always kuss between us). Such an unusual request in the ICU.

Incredibly, I didn't kuss him. "Don, I am not going to kuss you because I fear I am coming down with something. I do not want to give it to you." I was terrified that I was getting a cold and that I might give it to him.

My dream of Don last night was frighteningly clear.

I am standing at a winding stonewall of Fort Tryon Park, overlooking the Hudson River. The sky stretches far. I feel the

sensation of floating up. Suddenly wind rises and stirs me.
My spirit soars. I see Don up in the sky. He sends down mag-
netic power. I fly up with my arms stretched. I want to grab
Don and bring him down. But evasiveness fills me with fury.
I want to scream but no sound comes.

    "I want to bargain with you, Dai Sil," I hear Don's voice.

    "What kind of a bargain?"

    "If you agree to find repose from your frenzy to find me, I
will fly you up here once in a while."

    "Once in a while is not enough."

    "But you don't have to fly up here to see me. I am in your
heart all the time."

Today marks five months since Don left me.

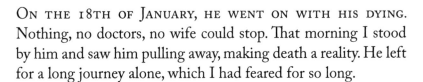

ON THE 18TH OF JANUARY, HE WENT ON WITH HIS DYING.
Nothing, no doctors, no wife could stop. That morning I stood
by him and saw him pulling away, making death a reality. He left
for a long journey alone, which I had feared for so long.

I found the following written in 2004.

    I have not taken care of my health and I don't wish
to die but I am especially concerned about my possible
death because of what it would mean to Dai Sil. It is
greatly painful to me that I am so helpless, so non-pro-
ductive, so burdensome. But what does she think? She
married a person whom she apparently loves and how
would that loss affect her life?

He wanted to know how my loss of him affected me. "Well,
Don, I'll tell you. It is infinitely worse than I had ever expected.

Don in 2004 on the way home from Toronto

I am nothing without you. Much of the time, life is unbearable without you. It is not worth living without you. I am a huge lump of sadness and despair."

I knew that Don wanted to come home from that hospital room more than anything in the world. I could not bring him home.

YESTERDAY I WAS OUT WITH VIRGINIA KASSEL. Virginia has been a friend since the1980s when I worked at National Endowment for the Humanities. She's a creator of *The Adams Chronicles*, a thirteen-part series which had the highest ratings ever on PBS. She invited me to see a play with her, *Accent on Youth*, at Manhattan Theater Club. In the middle of the day, I had an urge to go to the Strand Book Store. I left around 3 pm. I spent some time walking around Union Square, bought some apples and went to the Strand. After that, I had lots of time to kill before meeting Virginia at 7:30 pm. So I found a bar close to the Manhattan Theater Club. I had two glasses of white wine and read.

I thought of the writing I found on Don's computer just yesterday.

> *As I sit here at my desk overlooking the Hudson, reflecting on the past, my most cherished memories have to do with Dai Sil. I remember our courting at the fashionable Hay Adams Hotel with drinks there almost every evening. We decided to get married there. That was the greatest evening of my life. We parted early, because I had to head off to some meeting. I had been drinking our standard martinis—Bombay Gin, extraordinarily dry, straight up with an olive—but the intoxication I experienced had nothing to do with alcohol. It was the most thrilling, delightful, and significant intoxication of my life! I was so drunk with love.*

The play with Virginia was a comedy. I do not relate to comedies well. I think cultural differences emerge more with comedies than tragedies. What makes the American public laugh does not have the same effects on me. It signifies something then that Don and I laughed together at the same things.

Today is my 71st birthday. I am looking at Don's computer that generated a little piece of paper which he gave me on my 70th, the last birthday he had with me.

It is small and looks even fragile but it has all the power of Don's love expressed in his failing health.

Dai Sil
Happy Birthday
70 Ain't Too Bad.
Many More to Come
I love you
Don

ANOTHER SLEEPLESS NIGHT but something good happened last night. I watched a DVD which I had borrowed from my neighbor Ilyon, *My Architect: A Son's Journey*, by Nathaniel Kahn. The film captivated me. Powerful and inspiring.

All through it, I could not help but wish that Don were watching it with me. I don't remember what prompted us but we talked about Louis Kahn not long before Don's final trip to the hospital. We were both teary talking about the way a legendary architect collapsed of heart attack and was found dead in the downstairs men's room in Penn Station, Philadelphia. He died bankrupt and alone on the way back from India where he had been working on a project. His body lay unclaimed in the city morgue for three days because, for some inexplicable reason, Kahn had scratched out the address on his passport.

Despite his tragic death, Kahn left so many magnificent buildings behind him where his spirit still roams around. He died but his art will keep him immortal.

Don died. He left no buildings, paintings, and books, but he left undying love in me.

Love is greater than any immortal buildings.

Today I got a surprise call from Bea Beer, our neighbor who moved to Florida. She stressed that it was better that Don went first since I could cope with a life alone better than he. "Think about it, Dai Sil. How Don would be if he were left alone. Picture him living alone with that failing health." I had to see her point but still I wish Don stayed around a bit longer. Is this greed? Is this being selfish?

Now I'm going over a chapter he wrote in our joint "memoir," still in progress. It's on growing up on an Iowa farm. Through it I am getting to know a boy who started to drive a tractor and a truck at age 10, a boy who wrote an excellent essay and was accused by his classmates that he didn't write it because it was too good, a boy who became the president of his local 4H club and made it possible for women to join and vote. Whenever I read and work on his past, I feel both sadness and joy. I am getting to know him from his birth.

I have been reading wonderful books by Richard P. Feynman, a Nobel Prize winning physicist. I wonder if Don knew of him. I didn't. Born in 1918, he died of stomach cancer in 1988, at age 70, exactly the same age with Don when he died.

Friends Won Ok and Lo-I gave me an old paperback, *Surely, You're Joking, Mr. Feynman!* When I got home, I started reading it. What do I know about physics? Whatever he says will sound like Greek to me, I thought. But once I opened the book, I could not put it down. It was simply fascinating to follow the mind of a genius with heart, so eloquently expressed in humor. As I turned each page, I thought of Don. If he had not already read it, I know he would have enjoyed it immensely. He would have liked Mr. Feynman. And we would have enjoyed talking about him.

Don, high school senior

Feyman's first wife, Arline, died in a sanatorium while he was working on the atomic bomb at Los Alamos. She was his sweetheart from the tender age of youth. When he decided to marry her, she was already suffering from TB. Needless to say, his family was opposed to that marriage. Feynman wrote to his mother, "I want to marry Arline because I love her—which means I want to take care of her. That is all there is to it. I want to take care of her."

He wrote to Arline on June 6, 1945 (she died on June 16, 1945):

I am always too slow. I always make you miserable
by not understanding soon enough. I understand at last
how sick you are. I understand that this is not the time
to ask you to make any effort to be less of a bother to
others. Forgive me for my slowness to understand. I am
your husband. I love you.

When I read about Don on growing up on an Iowa farm,
it strikes me that what he lived with on that farm was a "restless longing." He was restless and longed for something but he
didn't quite know why "restless" and "what" he longed for. But
one thing is clear. That "restless longing" led him to leave the
beautiful sky of Iowa for the world beyond the corn fields.

The storm, maddening and fierce
Shakes the vast sea.
A lone sail boat is riding
Somewhere faraway.
A hypnotic ray rotates light and dark
And beckons the boat to stroke it,
As if the soft hair of a woman.

There must be a lighthouse
Not yet seen.

Morning dawns.
The sun is bright, air crisp.
A squirrel climbs a huge tree
On a farmstead
Looking down on a smiling boy
With his secrets of dreams and storms.
~ dskg

Don at 11 years of age

Once out in the world, Don learned that what he longed for was the world of ideas that can expand the human reality. But he kept the "restlessness" as a permanent state of his being. The very nature of the world of ideas made it impossible to get rid of "restlessness."

DON REMAINED RESTLESS UNTIL THE END. He read books even while in the ICU.

I found what he wrote during his trip to Iowa in 2003.

> _The greatest joy of my trip to Iowa was to revisit the land and the sky. Above all, the land is fertile. It is not flat, it undulates, rolls, endless small valleys and diminutive hills. One does not find waste land, with the exception of small creeks and gullies. In Iowa, one sees the bumps, but the sky still fills everything. Especially at night._

I was not with him when he took this trip. I was at the Pusan International Film Festival to show my film, _Wet Sand_. Before I left, we talked about his taking a leisurely car trip to Iowa by himself.

Reading about his delight with Iowan vistas, memories of our first trip out there together in the summer of 1979 stream back. He and I slipped out that first night after saying good night to his parents. Before I knew it, I felt like I was sitting on the clouds, traveling across the wide expanse of the starlit sky. The clouds were like waves in the ocean taking me beyond the limit of the sky. I held his hand and knew that he belonged to that sky. That night he taught me how to love the sky.

He and I both read _The Stranger_ by Albert Camus. I remember Camus' character, Meursault, discovering the blue sky in his cell three days before his execution. For the first time, in his 40 year life, he truly saw the sky through the skylight.

Now I am trying to see the sky every day.

MY THOUGHTS OF DON IN BED MELTED into a dream or a memory of a dream.

The cutest little boy about age 10 is holding a small pig. I stare at the boy and the pig. Soon I realize that the boy is Don on an Iowa farm. "Don, why are you holding that pig?"

"Oh, it's a runt. If left with her siblings, she might not survive. She's the weakest of the whole bunch."

"What are you going to do with her?" "I haven't figured that out yet. But I'm going to take care of her myself."

"Why do you love that runt?"

"Look at her. She is helpless but she already trusts me."

Today I am re-reading Don's writing entitled, "Why Memoir." I notice this time what Don stressed.

> *I married Dai Sil Kim, the finest decision I ever made by far. For, among other things, it rescued me from depression, which first inserted itself in my life while in Germany and returned again while I was working for the Congressman.*
>
> *Now I live in New York City, with limited energy, constant pain and great indecision about whether I should live or die. I fear I am a burden to Dai Sil and I think often that she would be far better off without me. I know she loves me but why should she have to bear this?*

Tears come down reading it. Silly man—why should she bear this? "I am not bearing anything. It is a fact of life. You are sick. I am your wife who loves you. There is no 'should.'"

Now it is year 2010. I find myself still immersed in the movie I watched last night, *The Road Home*, by Zhang Ziyi, a Chinese filmmaker I had adored until he made *Crouching Tiger, Hidden Dragon*. I think those "dazzling" special effects are killing the quiet soul of the movies, detracting from a touching plot and characters in their sorrow and joy.

The Road Home tells a simple story but soulful tale of love of a Chinese man and wife who were married in a small village, not arranged but fallen in love. The son who returns to bury his father is drawn into his mother's wish to carry her husband's body on foot for the burial. She believed that a body returned this way will never forget the road home.

Don will never forget the road home.

Today was a beautiful day. I went to Columbia Presbyterian for my B12 shot.

Well, as I walked home from Irving building, someone recognized me. It was Mr. Paris, the security guy at the Milestone building where we went three times a week for Don's physical therapy. He was the one who signaled us to come through without waiting in the line whenever I pushed Don's wheelchair inside. He was thrilled to see me and asked how I was. Then, one look at me, he understood. "How are you coping? You were so inseparable!" A security guy who noticed us together and understood our relationship from his own observation, "inseparable."

John Berger wrote:

> The opposite of to love is not to hate but to separate.
> If love and hate have something in common it is because,
> in both cases, their energy is that of bringing and hold-
> ing together—the lover with the loved, the one who hates
> with the hated. Both passions are tested by separation.

I am immersed in Kazantzakis' biography which his wife, Helen, put together mostly with his letters and journals.

> The more I love you, the more useless the world is to
> me because I can replace it with another, better, warmer,
> more simple world, as I would have created my entire
> life if I had been a Creator.

Don in 1980 at the Capitol Hill apartment

Don also wrote in 2004.

As I grow older, I increasingly want to be only with those I want to be with. It has been said of me more than once that I don't suffer fools gladly. At the time I wasn't at all certain that that was true, because I really did make efforts to deal with all who could help advance the cause I was then engaged in. And I don't regret that.

Now, I feel I don't have to indulge anyone.

Kazantzakis and Don—I was increasingly feeling like that, about Don, me and the world.

When I sat at our kitchen table with him in the evenings to eat our only shared meal, we counted on creating a world of our own as we journeyed toward our end. I think of what Kazantzakis wrote, "Everything inside my dark head was transformed into light and sun and love."

I remember asking Don a few times, "Don, if you do not want any social life, I would be happy to cut all of it. You must tell me honestly what you wish." I guess I raised this question more in 2008. Don did not give me a direct answer. Were I more sensitive, I should have known what "no answer" meant. *"Now, I feel I don't have to indulge anyone."*

Stars shining on the river,
With ripples of water
Are a spectacle of mystery.

A lone bird
Flies over a swamp in the field
To sit on a tree by the river.

A village widow
Sits under the tree,
The corner of her mouth
Dampened with saliva.

The stars,
The river,
The bird,
Send an alchemy
To the searing heart of the widow,
To seek comfort in life.
                    ~ dskg

I just finished reading a Korean novel, its title could be translated as *Take Care of Mom.*

Every line in the book is a deeply moving description of one woman's journey of unconditional, yet most profound human love, coupled with the thoughts and regrets of her husband, daughters and sons, to whom their mom and wife was fast becoming a forgotten woman. In the shocking state of their loss of mom and wife, they try to remember her love, the most miraculous love and yet consistently neglected and ignored, taken for granted as if it were their God given privilege.

The Mom who was accidentally left behind by her husband at the subway station, retains her love until that last journey into the faraway land, the land of no return, and yet she returned with her love. Her disappearance was her last gift of love to her children and husband. She turned their forgetting into memories of love. It was her disappearance that revives a miracle of life, a mother's love—devoted, pure and simple. Love, the only sure sign of immortality.

Reading the book, I thought of my mother and Don. He was totally with me when I struggled to give a semblance of dignity to my mother, who was suffering from Alzheimer's. He was there with me when my mother looked at me and said, "I don't know who you are but I like you. Like you a lot."

I think about the day when we buried my mother. A lot of things were said and done on that day. The most memorable for me was what Joshua, her great-grandson said, holding my hand. "Great-grandma's body was buried because her body no longer worked but her soul is up in the heaven. If she feels better up there, I wish she would come back here. I want to see her!" He was four years old.

Winter is here, the season of bare branches, snow and fierce wind.

I am reading Amos Oz's *The Same Sea*. He wrote, "What else can I say to you, sir, people are a riddle, even the ones you think you know best."

Still a couple hours before dawn.

I HAD AN OLD CLASSMATE FROM SEOUL who had a little crush on me. He came to see me when we lived at our 17th street house in D.C.. I took him to a near-by restaurant. Amazingly, he confessed, his mouth full of noodles, that he still loved me. Don was sitting at the house, a few blocks away. I smiled.

When I got back from lunch, Don's face lit up with a bright grin. Not a shadow of doubt or concern. His trust in me was complete.

So was mine in him. This makes me remember the time when an old girlfriend of Don's stayed with us. I was pissed at her once in a while because I had to work hard but was never jealous.

I found Don's email exchanges with a woman, Genelle, on whom he had a real crush, an older woman who taught French at Indianola High School while he taught German and World History.

Dai Sil and I came from such different backgrounds. Somehow, the marriage worked magnificently. Still does. So why? That is what we want to explore in our joint memoir.

He wrote that in 2004.

I found the following email I sent him in Don's AOL file, on September 1, 2008.

> Hi, Don,
>
> Over the years, our marriage worked because you were strong enough to let me be a stubborn, prejudiced, passionate but (hopefully) a caring person deep inside. In a way, our story is how an Iowa-born man married a North Korea-born woman, not because she is a submissive Asian woman, as the common stereotypic depiction goes, but defiant, strong woman who breaks the stereotype.
>
> In my old age, with a major cancer surgery behind and with a husband who suffers from pain that comes from everywhere in his thinning body, I am TRYING to look for inner peace by abandoning some of my obsessive ambition, work ethic, excessive need for right and wrong, etc. In your old age, worsened by your multiple health problems, you are turning into an insecure, sensitive man, (not in a good way), quick to anger, stubborn, etc. Much of the time, you are no longer there for me, allowing me to be me, I tell you—it is hard, if not impossible, to deal with this.
>
> I know I rambled but hope that you think about it. Some psychic transformation has to happen to you. DS

His answer:

"I accept your judgment. I believe you are correct. I will do everything I can to work on it." Yes, that was my Don. No nonsense Don.

Don often asked me about my strength as a child. We each had exacting young years that forged who we became. Perhaps both of us were given an abundance of responsibility.

HERE IS A TRUE STORY FROM WHEN I WAS 12 YEARS OLD. I told Don this story.

I was on a train headed to Masan from the port city Pusan. Somewhere in the north, the war was raging, brothers against brothers. In the late winter of 1951, I was sent to Pusan on the train from Masan where we the children lived with Mother and Grandmother. My father was in Pusan, trying to earn money to feed the family.

I was picked to carry out an important mission—to meet my father in Pusan and bring back the money he had earned. At the train station in Masan, my mother gave me stern instructions to sit still on one place until the train stopped at its final destination, Pusan. Then get off and look around. Father will be waiting. He will give me money and put me back on the train to come back to Masan. As long as I keep these instructions, nothing can happen and I will be safe.

I was scared but confronted with the enormity of my mission, I decided to show a cheerful disposition and confidence. "Please do not worry. I will be okay." I assured Mother.

Well, the train pulled into Pusan station, I found my father at the station right away. He took me to a small eatery, fed me some food and gave me an envelope tightly sealed. "Be careful. If you lose it, you will all starve at least for a month." I nodded, my eyes locking with his. Trust and confidence between the two of us were established. And he sighed a deep sigh of relief.

At the station, as my father helped me to get on, he gave me an assuring smile. No hugs, no kisses on the cheeks. We were not physical in our expressions of affection.

With a long whistle, the train moved toward Masan where I was to be met by my mother. I sat by the window, with my small bag on my lap, my hands clutching it tightly. I imagined my mother's smiling face and the faces of my siblings going after food on the table.

Shortly after the train took off, I was startled by a bright voice, "Is anyone sitting here?" A middle aged woman of some beauty asked, pointing to the empty aisle seat. "No. No one is sitting there." "Do you mind company?" "Oh, no, not at all. Please sit."

I sat still and quietly. After a while, she started a conversation. "You are a girl, not yet a teen. How come you are traveling alone?" "I had to go to Pusan to meet my father. It was an errand which my parents thought I could carry out. And I can, as you see. I am not scared at all. All I have to do is to sit tight and then get off at Masan. My mother will meet me there." "What a brave girl you are! I bet your parents are very proud of you." "I guess they are. I hope so."

I do not know when and how long. I must have dozed off. When I opened my eyes, I checked my bag. Thank goodness, it was still on my lap. The woman said she would be right back. That nature called. I nodded. Sitting alone, I checked my bag. The white envelope which my father had given me was gone. I frantically looked for it through the piles of other stuff in the bag. It wasn't there. It was gone. Tears came to my eyes and I had the strongest impulse to scream.

By that time, the woman was coming back. I sat still, willed my tears go away and took a deep breath. She sat right by me and asked, "Did anything happen? You look pale. Are you sick?" "No, I am not sick. I am okay. But something terrible happened!" "What?" "I lost the money my father gave me to take back home to my mother. Our family will starve at least for a month if I don't find it. I have no idea who could have taken it. As soon as we get off at Masan, I will report to the police. Aunt, (we children often called the strangers aunt), you are such a kind person. I am scared. Won't you stay with me until I report to the police when we get off?" "Of course, I will!" she said.

I had figured out that she was the only person who could have stolen my white envelope with money while I was dozing off. No matter what, I couldn't let her out of my sight. I had to keep her near me at all times until I could talk to police officers.

When we got off the train, I held onto her tight, as if my life depended on my grip. We walked together looking for the police. On our way, while I was looking away a bit, spotting two police officers walking toward us, I saw her dropping my father's envelope, which fell by my right foot. I stooped down to pick it up. When I stood up, the two police men passed by me and the woman was gone.

I opened the envelope and found the money.

It was the love that I felt for my family that kept my brain functioning with calm. At the sight of my mother, I broke down and sobbed. I handed the money to my mother and continued to sob.

YESTERDAY I WAS IN PITTSBURGH to show my film, *Motherland*, at a conference.

I believe the screening went okay. Coming into Pittsburgh airport to catch a flight back home, I saw a man sitting on a wheelchair. That triggered an image of Don on a wheelchair at JFK on September 29, 2004. We were headed to Germany for our 25th anniversary.

It was a trip filled with excitement and despair: Excitement for being together away from home in Germany with Don as my guide; but despair from his illness that kept him in a German hospital for ten days, with a doctor's warning that he might die. The darkest day of my life.

The other day I bought a small album for the photos from our trip to Germany. Don looked happy in those pictures. The last photo is one of Don and my nephew Paul outside the hospital on the day of his discharge. Don sits in a wheelchair and Paul stands behind him. Don looks even thinner than usual but a wicked grin is all over his face. I bet that smile not only reflected joy to be headed home, but also a plot somehow to persuade Paul to buy a pack of cigarettes so that he could sneak one!

Paul had been summoned to the Bavarian Alps where Don was hospitalized. He drove our rented car to Berlin, from where we flew to JFK. Don and I came home together, both alive. I'm so glad that we took that trip. I am even more glad that Don was happy that we took that trip.

Don wrote in July 2003:

> *Dai Sil has helped me enormously. She has stated, and I agree, that had she been with me when I was working on my dissertation in Germany, I would have finished it. It is quite interesting that I gained self-confidence after I married her and I advanced mightily in my career. She is an intellectual mate, a shoulder friend. We are perhaps above all best friends.*

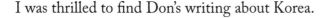

I was thrilled to find Don's writing about Korea.

> *I actually had a chance to go to Korea long before I met Dai Sil. When I was in Germany working on my doctoral dissertation, I became increasingly frustrated with the loneliness and isolation. That's when I took a job with the University of Maryland's Overseas Division, teaching American history to our soldiers on military*

bases in Mannheim and Heidelberg. Afterwards they offered me the same position based in South Korea, but I didn't accept for a variety of reasons.

Partially it was because my impression of Korea was based on a series of black-and-white images from television footage of the Korean War—bleak, dismal, dark. I am sure that sense of Korea I had in the 1970s was not far off from the facts. But Dai Sil transformed them into a rainbow of colors and heavenly feelings.

I finally had a chance to visit South Korea with Dai Sil in 1987. We were given the VIP treatment, thanks to Shilnil Park, a Korean diplomat I met while at NEH and who was, by then, back in Seoul.

Of all the things that we did, the most memorable was the three days Dai Sil and I spent in a Catholic cemetery on the outskirts of Seoul, while two hired workmen built a stone restraining wall around her grandmother's grave. I bonded with them on Korean wine, soju, and American cigarettes."

I dreamed of Don last night.

The sky is lavish with stars. Don and I are sitting together, our bodies attached as if twins in a womb. Emotion swirls not only inside of us but all around, locking us into a cosmos bursting with energy. "Where are we?" I ask Don.

"Does it matter where we are?"

"No, it doesn't as long as we are together." Somewhere I hear the sound of wind, that haunted sound.

"Do you hear that sound? It's almost time for me to go," says Don. I cling to him even closer.

"Dai Sil. Time for you to go back to the comforts of life for a while longer."

Autumn rice fields in Korea

This morning, as I passed by the bookcase in his room, my eyes were drawn to a black cane hanging on it, where Don had always left it. One day he asked me to bring his cane to the ICU. He took it from me, laid it across his chest, and put both of his hands firmly on top.

He wanted to get out of the hospital and walk! I will always keep that cane and see him walking alongside me.

In the year 2004, September 30 at Heathrow Airport. Don and I were scheduled to get on a flight to Berlin where we planned to celebrate our 25th anniversary on October 1.

We spent a night at an airport hotel in Heathrow to catch a flight in the morning. We were late. We had to get to the gate in a hurry. Don struggled to walk. Tears gathered in my eyes watching Don taking one step at a time holding onto his cane.

I told him that I would run and tell the people at the gate that he was behind me. He just nodded and I ran. The British Airways staff was more than understanding and told me to relax. They would wait for Don and I should also wait for him. I started running back to find him.

From a distance, I saw a man with a black cane, coming toward my direction. At that moment, I owned the sky, the sun, the moon, and stars, and everything in it.

Memories
Lay in silence
In my head, chest and soul.

Sometimes memories come
In a bulky layer,
Other times, one by one.

A memory comes now,
Shifting my sadness,
Into a spurious joy.

I remember crocuses,
Yellow and violet,
Lifting their heads,
Through the snow,

Quiet and beautiful,

Standing between each stone,
Lined up to make a path,
To our red front door.

That first winter,
Trying to awaken to Spring,
In the front yard of our white brick house,
On a tree lined street.

~ dskg

Iowa corn fields in the winter

Winter

O death, where is thy victory?
O death, where is thy sting?

1 Corinthians 15:55

Winter

If a bridge awaits him.
He will cross it.
If darkness makes him lost,
He will look for
The sun and the moon.
If sadness hovers over him,
He will summon euphoria.

The distant sound of a drum
That sings the litany of life
Will become louder and louder
And help him to betoken the love
I send with him.

> ~   *d s k g*

O N JANUARY 18, 2009, death invaded the lives of one old couple whose only wish was to grow older together.

On that day, the sky fell, and the earth stood still. I became a huge void, and the world became unreal.

When I returned to the apartment after seeing him last in his ICU room, never to see him again, dead or alive, I was calm. Don died and I was alive, but my life was as numb as a doornail.

The next day, Stella, my niece, and her husband, Chun Wei, and my sister, Dai Gook, came to accompany me to the funeral home. As I sat down, I asked Anne, the funeral home director, if she made sure that it was Don whom she picked up at the hospital, not someone else. She pulled out her phone from her bag and showed me a photo of Don. She must have taken it at least a few hours after he died.

It was Don. His face was remarkably calm, peaceful and even alive. Alive in death. I knew then that the photo was a message to me from Don that he was okay.

On the day of Obama's inauguration, which Don and I had waited for, I went to Woodlawn Cemetery to bid a final farewell to Don's body. Stella, Paul and Chun Wei came to pick me up. There was snow on the street. We followed Anne's direction and found the cemetery with ease.

The grave-yard was serene and lonely. We parked the car close to the chapel where Anne was to meet us. We were early. I walked on the ground a little, hoping that the door to the chapel was open, but it was closed. After a while, a black car pulled in, stopped, and Anne got out. Anne, with her driver, opened the back of her car and pulled out the box where Don lay. They would not open the box but gave me enough time to put my hand on it and whisper only to his ears. "Don, go in peace, but I am not saying good bye to you because you will always live with me."

A thought of him turning into ashes made me numb. Still no sting of death. I was oddly comforted that I too will turn into ashes one day and mine will be mixed with his.

Don and Dai Sil at the Wayside Inn in 2006

DON NEVER WENT ANYWHERE WITHOUT A CAP. He even wore a cap in the house except for the time he went to bed. He not only liked wearing a cap but his attachment to it became a need as he grew older and his health suffered. He needed the cap to keep himself warm and to cover his long grown hair. He was too weak to have hair cut as often as he needed or wanted.

I went to Korea in 2006 and brought him a unique cap, colored in natural persimmon dye. The color was not orange, not brown, perhaps somewhere in between. Don loved that cap. One day, I noticed that he didn't have the cap on his head. At one look at him, sadness darkened his face. "It was blown away by wind. I saw it blowing away but I could not chase it. No way I could chase it because of my shortness of breath. I just stood there and watched the cap blow away."

I wanted to hug him as if he were my little boy but I just

stood there and said, "Oh, Don!" I could not say another word. My heart was broken for him.

One evening, after taking a shower, Don announced with much pride, "Look Dai Sil, I took a shower. I even shaved. See!" He sounded like that little boy in an Iowa attic.

I remember the one time when Don came through the door, beaming. "You look different, Don," I said. "What is it? Oh, you had your hair cut! How did you manage it?" (I was planning to take him to a Korean barber shop across the George Washington Bridge for a haircut.) "Well, I walked to the same beauty salon where you get your hair cut on 187 Street. A Hispanic woman sat me down and cut my hair!" "Oh, that's Adele, the same woman who cuts my hair." "Yes, I know. We talked about you."

The pride and joy lit up his face, the face I so loved, so engrained in my heart. It was amazing how a little haircut gave him such a monumental sense of achievement.

> *A torrent of sadness comes,*
> *Yet light and stillness*
> *Inhale and exhale love.*
>
> *This is not a mere rarity,*
> *But a miracle*
> *That does not surrender*
> *To darkness.*
>
> ~ *dskg*

ANXIOUS TO GET BACK TO OUR MEMOIR, I search for Don's writings and come up with a file that was titled, "Some Intense Moments with Dai Sil." At the top of the list:

> **The day our friend Miae died. We were at their home;**
> **it was in the morning. We had recently transferred**

her from Calvary Hospital in the Bronx, a facility for terminally ill cancer patients. She was in her room on the second floor. As she was dying, tears flowed down her cheeks. It was as if she knew what was happening. I am pleased I was there, though, agonized by what occurred.

That writing hits me hard. From the time when Miae was told that she might have three weeks to live until the day she passed away after almost a year of excruciatingly painful treatments for tumors in her brain, Don was with me and with her every step of the way. Don's own health was not good but still he accompanied me every day. When she was at Calvary Hospital, the waiting station to die, she pleaded with me to ask Don to work on taking her home. "In many ways I trust Don more than you. He is a good man. I know he can help me go home!" I told Don this at the time. And I am glad I did.

I think of Miae's death and think of "They lie down alike in the dust, and the worms cover them." (Job, 21:26)

The death of my mother, the fire, Don's health crisis, then losing my best friend, Miae, to cancer, all happened in a span of a few years, 2001 to 2004. It felt like tragedy flooded my heart, like rain pouring in, and made me feel wet with sadness beyond my control. The sadness turns into unbearable emptiness when I remember what Miae said on one afternoon in early 2004, lying on her bed at Calvary, "I wonder how long it will take worms to eat me up!"

Yesterday, I could not write. I just went over every detail on that morning of Don's departure. Why did I not squeeze his hand as hard as I could and ask him to squeeze me back if he felt me? Why did I not put my head on his body and wail when the doctor declared him dead? Why did I whisper to him, not speak to him loudly, to make sure that he heard me?

I sat as if my soul went out of my body in the company of silent tears streaming down my cheeks.

Today marks three weeks of Don's passing. As I walked one block on Cabrini Boulevard, I saw him leaning against the wall. Then he wasn't there. I was so afraid to walk by Bleu, a local restaurant, Don's last hangout place. I felt as if he would stand there waiting for me with his cane. Then the Hilltop Pharmacy where he had gotten so many prescribed medicines.

I waited at a bus stop in front of that pharmacy. I saw him sitting on a bench waiting for me, which he sometimes did. The M4 bus stopped and brought me back to the most unreal reality, that he was not sitting on the bench and that he won't ever sit there waiting for me to pick him up. I rode the bus and got off at 112 Street and Broadway and walked to St. John the Divine on Amsterdam.

When I returned home, I was exhausted. As I entered the apartment, I said, "Hi, Don, I am back!" but no response in his grainy voice, "It's about time." Only a total silence.

If I were still a believing Christian, I could insist that "Christ conquered death. Like him, we can make our death into a new birth. We can strip the power of death over us by sticking to a risen Lord."

Alas, I don't have strong enough faith to rejoice Don's death and look forward to my death because Christ rose from the dead. Nevertheless, something moves me to write:

> *Hold onto the vastness of the universe*
> *With single-minded devotion.*
> *Don't let glory glide by you.*
> *It's our invisible, our lofty salvation.*
>
> ~ *dskg*

Sleep did not come to me last night. The more I tried to sleep, the wider my eyes opened.

The day hardly started but I was already tired. I gathered all the energy I could muster, walked to my computer room; I read what Don wrote, "From American Way to American Dream."

As I read on, I was again astounded that we both started out to rely on Christian God to lead us to what we were looking for in life.

I thought of how a goodly part of my life was spent in search of a God I could believe in. When I married Don, he was not a church-going Christian. We didn't argue about God, because Don knew that I was capable of defining my own God. It was good enough to him that I wasn't blindly looking for a dogmatic certainty. He had the deepest respect for people's honest search for truth. I also knew that his faith in God, however he defined it, was purer than I could find in any pulpits of the churches. I knew that his belief in God was very close to that of his pantheistic father whom he so loved. Don saw God in every thing.

We didn't talk much about our beliefs about an afterlife. I was thrilled to find his writing:

> *For myself, I hope to die in my sleep or in some other totally unobtrusive manner. Then I want to be cremated with my ashes simply thrown into the wind. We live our lives as best we can. When we die it is over and we should get out of the way for others to live, leaving no burden upon them. Expensive burials from a Christian perspective—a perspective I no longer share—should be anathema. The body is only the physical vessel of the soul. When the body dies, the soul endures in another form.*

Evening. I sit on his empty bed for a while and finally pick up the *New York Times* outside of our door, most of which will probably be unread. Since his passing, I had been unable to read the paper and watch the news. Politics, especially the politics of the Obama administration, reminded me of his absence so much that I could hardly bear them.

Back to his room, on his bed, I remember how I became super-critical of America and its imperialism over the years, especially during the Bush administration. He would say, "Dai Sil, now, now. You speak as if you were not an American. You are an American, not by virtue of your birth like me, but by choice." I flash a sad smile remembering how my sharp criticism of America sometimes got on his nerves, to put it mildly. One day, however, he stood by the kitchen counter and said, "I've never thought I would say this but right now I wish I lived anywhere but in America. What the Bush administration is doing to this country is unbearable!"

I drag myself to his computer and find a file that said, "American Dream." I read it before but today, re-reading, I see more of his anguish about Bush than before. Here's what he wrote:

> *I write because I am in profound despair about the United States and the American Dream. The nation has become, as Senator J. William Fulbright warned us during the Vietnam War, arrogant with power. Our President, George W. Bush, is in full war cry. While his justifications for the war on terrorism shift along with the circumstances from harborers of terrorists to a direct military threat to the American people, he remains consistent on one point. He claims to know what is just and pure. He boasts of moral clarity.*
>
> *It is his version of the American Dream and he'll readily impose it on any nation or person that is not living by those standards. His claim is philosophically bolstered by the devotees of Leo Strauss, the German expatriate who taught at the University of Chicago and who has inspired an influential cadre. His was the assertion of the American Empire in the 21st Century. Because this nation has been successful and is now unquestionably the dominate power in the world.*

We have, through the moral clarity of George W. Bush, arrogated unto ourselves the right to impose our will wherever we wish. I doubt though that George W. has ever heard of, and certainly has never read, Leo Strauss.

I felt consoled that Don went away at least knowing that G.W. Bush would not be in the White House but Obama would be.

Last night, a dream, as best I can recall:

I am looking for Don in a corridor—long, empty corridor, bereft of any furniture, empty, not even a small stool. Surging of fear makes me shaky but I walk through it, my legs steady, eyes open and ears perked, only to end at a back door of a dark building. I step outside and find trees.

The wind rustles the leaves in the trees and beckons me to come. There, behind a huge trunk, Don stands, his face in shade but without any nuance of irritation or irreverence which he sometimes had when in pain. His face is creased with laughter. "I am glad you found me." I hear Don's voice. Suddenly, I feel reticent, gladness filling my heart.

I want to put my head in his chest and cling to him.

"Dai Sil, there is my hawk. He came to let me fly with him." "Wait, I want to fly with you." "Not yet," and he flies away with the hawk before I could stop him.

A MONTH AGO TODAY, I LOST DON in the ICU of Columbia Presbyterian Hospital. For an entire month, he has been gone but I still can't believe that he is gone.

C.S. Lewis wrote in his journal that grief feels like fear. Though one is not afraid, the sensation is like being afraid. I understand what he means. When I get up, my body feels lost, as if it does not know where to locate itself, where to hide from the fact that Don is no longer here. My body is afraid. I am saturated with fear. I have fear of another day of looking for Don, only to fail.

I go to his room and sit on his bed. Eerie quiet. His chair is still by his bed. Don always put the chair close by him when he went to bed at night as a tool to move himself around, to reach the desk, computer and bathroom. I remember how he did everything to make himself function with minimum help from me. He was proud to figure out the way to use that chair as a means of mobility. It took so much effort for him to stand up and walk.

His room is still nice and clean and waiting for him. I am still charging his cell phone which he always put within his reach every night when we said good night to each other. In my head I know that he is gone but I have to find him.

What is death? Not even death could have taken him away from me. Don would not leave me alone. He had to be around. It was up to me to find him.

I read in some book about children under the age of five, how they take death. That they do not recognize death as an irreversible fact. Not only that, in death they see life and attribute life and consciousness to the dead.

Never mind the children. I was a 70-year-old woman with a Ph.D in religion but I did not recognize death, perhaps death as an end of someone's life, but not Don's! He could not be dead. He was alive and around somewhere. I must find him.

Maybe death
Isn't darkness, after all
But so much light
Wrapping itself around us.

Mary Oliver

The shapes and modes of my grief and pain are quite varied. Today as I try to find Don, my grief feels like soft clouds and warm blankets that embrace my entire body, sending quiet shivers.

I think about what makes me so sad. I believe it is compassion I feel for the suffering Don endured and loneliness he felt.

Some might say that what Don endured was light in comparison with many others who suffered and are still suffering. That can be a helpful perspective but never enough to take away my sorrow. He was the singular human being who gave me meaning of life with his undying love, even when he was dying, and whom I loved with my soul.

Death is a universal phenomenon which no one can escape and yet we so rarely talk about it, to the extent that many write about keeping "deadly silence" about death. Why?

I can only try to answer the question for myself. Obviously, I could not accept that Don will die but in all candor, it was not so much for Don but for myself that I could not bring up death. I must have believed that if I talked about death, it would hasten to bring about my most dreaded fear, the fear of losing him. I could not face my life without him.

I never feared anything more in life than Don's death. I could not talk about it. People write about how no one can accept or think about one's own death. For me, I could not think about Don's death.

He can't die as long as I am alive. It was not love. It was being selfish. It was greed that I didn't allow Don to talk about his death. He was the one who was facing it. He must have wanted to tell me a few things but I didn't let him.

Just a couple of days before he was gone forever, I heard him say, mixed in thick groans, "I do not think I can go on much longer." It was a cry of pain and agony. Perhaps a plea as well for me to help him go. His will to live was strong; that I did not and do not doubt, but the body that imprisoned his will was failing with added pain every hour. Even then, I was not really thinking of his pain. I was thinking of me. I was not ready to let him go. I wanted him to fight. I wanted him to live. If I prayed to God, the God of my childhood, it was not "Thy will be done." I prayed what His will should be: to give Don more time on earth. Not to take him away from me.

I am obsessed about death. One of the most dominant ideas about death: it is simply a doorway to another life, usually called eternal life.

More Westerners are familiar with the Judeo-Christian teaching about death as a doorway to either heaven or hell. In this case, time is linear and life and death are a one time deal. But there are millions of people who think and believe that life is a single chapter in a book and that death is a transformative experience, not the end. These views are usually held by those who believe in re-incarnation, in many lives, not just one life.

We find the following in *Still Here*, in *Emmanuel's Book*.

> Even when you are dead,
> you are still alive.
> You do not cease to exist at death,
> That is only illusion.
> You go through the doorway of death alive
> And there is no altering of consciousness.
> It is not a strange land you go to
> But a land of living reality
> where the growth process is a continuation.

In the same vein, Dalai Lama has this to say about death:

> I hold the view that death is rather like changing one's clothes when they are torn and old. It is not an end in itself. Yet death is unpredictable—you do not know how

Don in Iowa in late 1960's

it will take place. So it is only sensible to take certain precautions before it actually happens.

My thoughts are back to two weeks at the end of 2008, the two weeks between hospitalizations. Don was hospitalized in December 2008 for a flu which nearly killed him. We were fully prepared to spend Christmas at the hospital but, thank God,

Don was discharged on December 24. We were thrilled to be home at the special season of the year. Just the two of us at home away from hospital and other gatherings.

We spent a quiet Christmas Eve with a glass of wine reading our thoughts in each other's eyes. Between December 24 and January 3, 2009, we both did things with tender disposition and hearts with overflowing gratitude. We didn't talk much. We looked in the eyes of the other and knew that we were blessed. Don's mind was unusually alert and his disposition gentler during those two weeks at home. Neither of us suspected anything, especially what we feared most, separation from each other. We just savored each moment. Perhaps, he was preparing to take his long journey but Don showed nothing but blissful joy of being alive with his wife.

I COME ACROSS MY JOURNAL ENTRY, JANUARY 1, 2009. "I consider the first day of 2009 a blessed one. Don and I are still alive!" On January 1, I had no idea that only on the 3rd, I would be taking Don to his final trip to the hospital, never to come back.

I do not fight my grief. The grief will always be with me. But I do second-guess things. Millions of small and large things I could have done differently. Was there anything I could have done to prolong his life? Or to lessen his suffering? Anything that added extra burden to his life that was so full of pain and suffering? I even wonder if any of the food I made him eat caused his internal bleeding.

RIGHT NOW, I AM THINKING OF JANUARY 3RD, 2009. The morning I took Don to his final journey to the hospital.

That morning, I found Don sitting up, but his head down, and shoulders drooped. I grabbed him, terror stricken. He was in terrible shape, his face darkly ashen. With total darkness descending upon me, I said, "Emergency 911?" "Not yet," he said. Well, we lost precious ten minutes before I called 911. By then, he was turning into an image of what might come. A shadow of death.

In all the years when we went through so many ambulance rides and life and death crises, he never said "dying," not even in the Bavarian Alps where a German doctor told me to prepare for the worst. However, that morning, with his head in my chest, he said, "I am dying. Let me die."

I am struggling with the memory of that moment, still so vivid and alive. I remember what I did. I begged him, "Not yet, not yet. Don, please. It is not time yet for you to go. Please stay alive a bit longer, please, please, for me."

Oh, even I know there was no way that I would not have called 911. However, when he said, "I am dying. Let me die," I could have buried his head in my chest and gently rocked it instead of begging him to live for me. I could have understood his long struggle with failing health and helped him to let go his will to hang onto his body, ready to give out. Instead I begged him to live for me. I could have helped him to escape 16 long days of pain and suffering in the ICU of Columbia Presbyterian Hospital.

I pushed him, pushed him all the while he was struggling with so much pain and agony. I put pressure on him to feel better and to live long, longer than his ailing body could support him. What kind of a caregiver was I if I didn't even allow him to be sick?

"Don, please forgive me. Can you hear me?"

Toward the end of Don's life, I could hardly count the pills the doctors and their nurses gave him. I could not count the tests Don was subjected to. Somewhere from the depth of my soul, I heard a voice, "Who can guarantee that all that stuff pushed into his system will not finally kill him, not save him?" So all the while clinging to those doctors to perform a miracle so that I could bring my Don home yet one more time, I feared deep inside what was going on in that ICU.

I hear me telling myself. "Dai Sil, know that Don came to this world, met you and lived his life with you as long as the natural order of cosmos designed for him allowed. What's more, Dai Sil, don't think of death as your enemy but as a friend which liberated Don from his old age, coupled with sickness, both of which Don hated.

"Death is neither cruel nor merciful. It just is. Death just as 'is' will also come to you. And when it does, you are in luck because it will open the door to enter where Don waits for you."

I sigh a deep sigh and experience a momentary relief.

> *I want to be able to say*
> *At my death bed*
> *"I loved" and*
> *"I lived"*
>
> *No more, no less.*
>
> *Oh, one more*
>
> *"I am happy because I am*
> *Going where Don is"*
> *~ dskg*

On that first day at ICU, I stayed in the hospital with Don, and then the next morning, I went back to our apartment briefly for a shower and change of clothes. I returned to the hospital around 9:30 am but they would not let me in until 12 noon. I am haunted by the hospital scenes.

Those faces, full of anguish,
Fight against death.

All those faces are caught in the upheaval
Of hope and despair.

As the shadow of death spreads darker
And wider, some curl up,
Their eyes closed.

Others look upward,
Seeking serenity in the violent silence.

~ *dskg*

Just as I tried to calm myself, I find this on Don's computer.

It has now been six months since I collapsed with severe breathing problems in a small town in Germany. Taken to the emergency room in Berchtesgaden, a doctor told Dai Sil the first evening that I was likely to die. I didn't. I am pleased; I think Dai Sil is as well.

I scream at Don with rage.

"I think Dai Sil is as well." What's that? "How could you be so cavalier about it? Didn't I tell you how the German doctor brought me the darkest moment of my life; how she cut my heart into thousand pieces?" I was so mad and sad that I wanted to kill Don. Alas, I could not even do that. He was already dead!

All the while death was approaching Don, he and I clung to each other. I thought I was helping Don but looking back, it was Don who tried to help me, giving me moments in which I could help him. He wanted to leave me something that I could hang onto.

My mind was once again preoccupied with a recurring question: "Why is Don dead and why am I alive?"

I knew Don wanted to live. Period. I was/am not sure if he even thought about who should go first. He just wanted to stick around a bit longer, the two of us together. But his body gave out and he had to go.

If death means the end of the individual as he existed, the end, nothing else, no more consciousness, nothing like soul, spirit, THE END, then he does not even know he is dead. So he can't be sad or anything else. This means my sadness is mostly for me, not for him. He does not know anything. So he is okay. True that he didn't like not knowing but it is no longer up to him to know. He is not capable of wishing.

If death means the body is gone but his soul/spirit/intellect fled from his body and is alive, he is indeed liberated from ailing body that gave him all that pain and suffering. His spirit is with God, however we define God. I can't imagine Don not being with God. He was not a practicing Christian or a religious person, but I cannot think of any person who more deserves to be with God than he. This calls for "rejoicing" instead of being sad. This means he is with me in spirit and we are together, his spirit guiding, protecting and loving me. So either way, I should be able to face his death and go on living with him.

Then why don't I feel better?

I say "Good morning, Don,"
As I get up to start a new day
And I hear,"Good morning, Dai Sil."
Honest, I hear it
But no pulse in that voice

I walk to his room
His bed empty, his black chair
Staring at me, also empty
I put him in his chair
Honest, I see him
But no gentle hand touching me

I stand in anguish
With primal sorrow
Soon to turn into fury
For leaving me alone
He knew damn well that
I didn't want to live alone

~ dskg

There was lots of confusion for both of us. It was understood that he wanted to lead a normal life as much as he could, not a life of an invalid. He wanted to think of himself as a person with some health problems, a sort of an understatement, to put it mildly, not a "sicky." I wanted to respect that. And in so doing, I often lost delicate balance. The same thing also happened to him. Further, both of us failed to understand fully the way illness could distort people's behavior. He was worried about losing his mind. He did not lose his mind, but his emotional balance was influenced by the illness. Neither of us took that into full consideration.

Last night a garbled dream:

I am in a subway station, running up the stairs—long and steep stairs. Don is at the bottom, looking up. "Hurry up, Don. I don't want to be late for the play!" I do not understand why he is just standing there. Then, it hit me. "Of course, Don can't climb up those stairs. Look at him. He is panting, short of breath. He has trouble just standing! "Dai Sil, you are such an insensitive bitch." I reprimand myself.

Then I see Don walking on a two-lane road, stretched far beyond what my eyes can see. He is walking alone. He must be going on a long journey. Suddenly, a terrible fear grabs me. "He is never going to walk back on the other lane. How come Don is not taking me with him? Did we not promise each other that we will always travel together wherever we go?"

I am in my bed, and listen to the clock clicking. Where is Don? It is late. I try to feel Don on his side of our bed. He is not there. His absence frightens me to death. Then suddenly, I feel Don, chattery, ebullient, pulling me close to him and saying, "I had to take a one-way journey alone. But I can climb all the stairs and ride subways with you." "But I don't want any of that. I just want you here, right now!"

When I finally opened my eyes, I didn't know if I wanted to be in that dream or wake up to another day without Don.

I wake up with hope in my heart that today I might have a normal day, whatever that means. I make coffee and sit by my computer. I open Don's file and find:

We have another challenge in my retirement. I tended to be divided in my personality; aggressive at work, passive at home. That worked well for me psychologically. Now, in retirement, I tend to become frustrated when Dai Sil consistently takes charge, commands control of any situation. I command control, it seems to me, in nothing.

Oh, my, it never ends. I am beyond being shocked. I sigh. I knew that retirement was hard for Don but didn't understand its depth. I thought I was just doing what I had always done: to be in charge at home. Sometimes, perhaps, more than I used to, because I felt compelled to make sure that I do all I could. I did not want him to do things at home in his frail health.

Now I understand why he got so upset whenever I took over things he seemed to have trouble with, even with a little task like opening a wine bottle! I was naïve or insensitive. Whichever was the case, I hurt Don. How could I be so totally blind that I was becoming a problem to him?

I walk around the apartment aimlessly. After a while, I settle back in front of the computer. I find more of Don's writings and read that he contributed nothing to our marriage, to our relationship and that he should end quickly with his death. I nearly faint, unable to breathe, but there is more. He thought I deserved much better and he hoped I would find it once he was gone.

"Oh, my." I feel devastated. As if that was not enough, he wrote that he wanted to live until his father died so that his father would go in peace knowing that he was still alive and that I could inherit his father's money.

"Don," I scream, well, a quiet scream, lest my neighbors think I should be sent to an asylum. "I know you are dead but if your spirit lives, please get it in your thick head. I never worried about getting your father's money! All I wanted was you, you alive! That is the truth."

What a normal day I was having!? Is any day ever going to be normal for me?

I try to calm my nerves, determined to make today count, perhaps by getting away from the dark shadow of death. I open my apartment door. I thought I heard some sound outside. I find a huge box. I know what it is, our urn.

I ran downstairs to catch the Federal Express man who brought it up. He had already moved closer to 187 Street. I gave the man a generous tip for bringing it to our home.

I had put off opening the little black box that contained Don's ashes until I had a home for them. I worked on that urn with a sculptor in New Mexico. We went through an elaborate art piece somewhere in the middle of the process, and ended up with a simple stone house.

I actually got some help from Mr. Woo, Ilyon's father, an accomplished architect. His idea was to make a simple home, an unassuming but elegant home. He even sent me two models that looked like two boxes, but their proportions followed the golden rule of architecture and classic paintings. The urn was designed for two, with our names carved on the cover, so that my ashes would join his before someone throws them in the wind.

I did not have a heart to open it by myself. I waited until my friend Gail came to help me. It was quite a challenge to open that huge box but it was even more difficult to open the black box that had Don's remains. When we finally opened it, there were charcoal gray ashes in a plastic bag. That was Don, his ailing body reduced to ashes. I trembled holding him and I am still trembling.

Wedding rehearsal dinner

Our meeting,
A man and a woman
From two different worlds
Was a gift of the universe,
A gift astonishing and splendid.

Your disappearance
Sent a pang in my heart
Like an icy river.

But we did not bid
Farewell to each other.
The Universe will navigate us
To meet again and ignite new life.

~ *dskg*

I am working on a document for a coming screening of my film, *Motherland*, at Union Seminary on April 28th, a commitment I had made long ago. I am going over my bio and at the end, I find the mention of our joint memoir. I change "my husband" to "my late husband." It breaks my heart. "Late husband."

What day is it today? Must be a few days after April 10th, 2009. This morning, I make myself look at some papers on our finances.

I heard so many horror stories about widowed women who were left in such financial chaos that they had no time or energy to mourn the death of their husbands. But not Don. I remember it was one of those days at the end of 2008, shortly after his hospitalization, December 20-24, that he typed up details of our finances—bank numbers, stocks, and pension income—and printed it out for me. I could not look at it right away but when I finally did, I was amazed that he had worked out everything in such a way that we would each have an almost equal amount of monthly income after one of us died.

I came to him with that piece of paper. I wanted to tell him how thoughtful he was but had hard time saying it. He looked at me and said, "Dai Sil, are you finding it difficult to say the word, 'death'? Try the word, 'pre-deceased.'" At that we both relaxed and laughed.

If and when stocks go up, I am going to figure out a way to honor Don with that money. I know we had agreed to leave whatever money we have when we both die to feed the starving children. However, while I am still alive, if I can rescue the money in stocks, I plan to do something to honor him. Maybe scholarships for a few high school students each year. He wrote more than a few times that he should have remained a high school teacher. For instance, there was a letter that he wrote to his Dad, dated May 6, 1995.

I still believe strongly in the democratizing power of public education. I still think that the best thing I have done in my life was high school teaching. Perhaps I should have stayed there. Every year, I hear from a few former students who speak kindly of their experiences in my classroom.

Yes, I do know how passionate he was about public education. One of his all-time favorite quotes came from William Butler Yeats, "Education is not the filling of a pail, but the lighting of a fire."

At least he believed that he lighted a fire for some of his high school students. If only he knew for how many others he lighted fires! They were not just his high school students!

Today, with these thoughts, life replaced death for a while.

Will I not stop looking for Don, even in my night mind?

Don and I are walking on the beach, looking at distant waves coming toward us. We both stop almost simultaneously to see sand dunes piled high. Words tumble out of our lips as if in chorus, "How magnificent!" Then I hear Don say, "These days my body feels like sand." I do not ask, "What do you mean?" I keep quiet.

A long silence, both of us preoccupied. "Don, what are you thinking?" I finally break the silence. "My health," he says with abandon. Suddenly, I see immense loneliness piercing his thin body like a sharp knife. Feelings—deep, deep feelings—well up in me and stir my soul, "Oh, God, don't take him away from me!"

Don is already in the water walking toward the sun that's starting to fade. I lurch after him, stretching my arms to reach him.

APRIL 18, 2009. IT HAS BEEN THREE MONTHS since Don left me. Memories of the time right before they started getting ready for Don's surgery flood around me and I experience a sinking sensation. I grab the kitchen table as if I were holding on a straw in the vast ocean.

Before they took Don to the operating room, Mark, his nurse practitioner, told me to go inside and talk to him. "If you wish to say something to him, now is the time." I went in and said, "You wish to go through the operation, don't you? Please, please tell me." He muttered something which made no sense to me. He had told me that I was not a good listener, a couple days before in the ICU. I tried to hear him but I could not understand what he said. Probably, he didn't say anything coherent. He was already so heavily sedated and extremely agitated. I had to give up on a two-way talk. I did say loudly and clearly to him. "Don, I am never going to say good-bye to you, because you are coming back to me alive. Be brave."

> *Every day I think of what I would say*
> *If I had a moment with him again*
> *If I could say just one sentence*
> *It is always, "I love you."*
>
> *I had said it all*
> *So did he, in his husky voice*
> *The only thing we didn't say*
> *Was "good-bye"*
>
> ~ *dskg*

Death could not part us.

EARLY MORNING OF APRIL 24, 5 AM. For the past few days, I have been thinking about almost nothing but weather. Don's Memorial Gathering is tomorrow and I plan to hold it at the apartment complex park.

After checking and double-checking the weather forecast, I am finally convinced that weather is going to be fine. Tomorrow, according to the *New York Times*, it is going to be about 84 degrees with occasional patch of clouds. Well, I had delegated Don to be in charge of the weather. He is coming through.

In anticipation of friends coming to our apartment after the Memorial Gathering, I decided to get on my knees with wet rag to clean the corners of his room, going through all those wires around his computer. From the tangle of white wires out popped a silver pen!

Not too long before his final journey to the hospital, Don asked me to search for a silver pen among the wires. "Dai Sil, I just dropped one of my favorite pens, a thin silver pen. Would you see if you can find it?"

Well, this morning, it showed up and I was excited and said out loud, "Don, look what I found!" only to realize that Don was not there. My heart sank. But I managed to place his pen on his computer table and continue cleaning. I am determined to stay strong for tomorrow.

Will the Memorial tomorrow make me accept Don's death?

In a twilight sleep, my mind wanders and moves in and out of memory.

It is winter. Snowflakes are on the bare branches of shivering trees. Don stands against a huge tree trunk, wearing a Burberry tweed coat that I had bought for him on sale (still

$400 on sale in the mid 1980's), his neck wrapped in a color-
ful, long scarf, which I had bought at Nieman Marcus, also
on sale. Each time I announced how much I saved by buying
expensive items on sale, Don gave a roaring laughter. I knew
what went through his mind, "Oh, she is so full of it but so
cute. I will keep her for eternity."

I want to go close to him, longing for his arms to hug me.
Not to summon lust but to feel sensuous joy. But suddenly
darkness falls, making my eyes blind with sadness. My heart,
lonely and grieving, plummets into a barren land, and I
stand in a moment of stillness. I sit up to an enlarged photo of
Don. I want to go back to my thoughts. There I can still hope
that he will come to me.

APRIL 28, 2009. Three nights passed since Don's Memorial Gathering on Castle Village Garden. For three nights, I could not sleep. So many had hinted that the Memorial would/should give me some release from pain and sadness. However, on the morning of 26th of April, I felt as if my sadness and the pain were tripled. The Memorial did not perform a miracle or magic in that sense, but I must write for the record that it was a glorious tribute to Don.

April 25th was a day of full sunshine. Actually, there was too much sunshine. Someone commented, "Don is playing a little joke on us. Well, Don did with a chuckle, 'Okay, Dai Sil, you wanted sunshine. Here it is. I will make sure that there is a little more than you need.'" It got a bit hot but otherwise it was perfect weather, with occasional breezes from the river.

The garden was beautiful. Green grass covered the ground, tulips were in full bloom and there were still some forsythia, the yellow spring flower which Don was fond of calling by its a Korean name, *gaenari*.

I had enlarged a picture of Don leaning against a huge tree in front of his brother's house in Iowa which I took in the mid

1980s. I put that picture on a stand. In front of it was a large vase which contained 200 white roses, roses from me for Don! We put chairs to face the Hudson River, GW Bridge and Palisades Park. Don and roses faced the audience. The setting was simple and gorgeous the way I hope he would have wanted.

To me, that photo represented an Iowa farm boy grown to be a decent man, leaning against a tree looking out far beyond that lovely Iowa field but never failing to give that unforgettable grin to a woman whom he had married.

Everyone covered different aspects of him and his life but a theme emerged—he was one hell of a decent human being with a generous heart, respect for each individual stemming from a profound belief in humanity, coupled with magnetic physical presence and a brilliant mind. Friends talked about his having an electricity about him and his body often barely containing its energy. There is no question that he accomplished an awful lot: what he did was brilliant, pioneering and impressive.

Sue Kaul expressed best how pioneering he was when she said, "Don did things in the 1960s for his campaign work that Obama did in 2007 and 2008." Yes, they were all proud of what he accomplished but even more enduring for them was who he was. What a unique human being he was with compassionate heart.

As I had worked on the Memorial, however, I rarely felt that I was doing it alone. He was with me. There were many who helped but none more than his friends in our neighborhood. I had not known them. I had not joined his gatherings in our local bars. In the spirit of what we had always done in our marriage, respecting privacy and independence of each other, I wanted those gatherings to be his private world. I delighted when he was able to take a walk, a few steps at a time, resting often. He sat with his friends and came home with stories to tell. When those friends learned that he was never to join them again, they became my friends and helped from the beginning to the end to remember their friend. It was as if Don asked Peter, Mark and Harold to help me.

MORE THAN HALF OF JUNE IS ALREADY BEHIND US. Close to lunch time, I thought to do something drastic, to help myself. I drove to Tae Hee's place (my long time college friend from

Korea) to have lunch with her and my elementary school chum, Kang Ok. They have been trying to help me out of the depth of their caring hearts.

Tae Hee's repeated mantra since Don's passing has been, "Look at me. I lost my husband when he was only 43 to a lung cancer. You remember Dr. Chang, a brilliant chemist. He died at the peak of his career. Don lived to be 70. Think about it."

Then Kang Ok joined in, "Remember me? I lost my husband to a liver cancer when he was 59."

Yes, I appreciate both Tae Hee and Kang Ok. They want to help me put Don's death in a perspective. I do not deny the value of doing that but each loss is unique, just as each relationship is unique.

Don to me was and remains to be a singular human being. If his life was unique for me, so was his death. The fact that death is universal does not make every death the same. Each death is different and has to be understood as such. Further, I do not know of anyone who thinks death is okay because everyone dies.

If individual life is sacred, so is death. We must learn to pay respect to the dead and place death at a rightful place. If each mourning has to be understood as unique to the individual grieving, each death has to be respected.

Almost two decades ago, I made a film about the Los Angeles riots, the riots in which lots of African Americans and new immigrants were pitted against each other, especially between African Americans and Korean immigrants. In that film, I feature the death of a nineteen year old Korean man and his mourning mother.

At a screening of that film at the Human Rights Festival in New York City in 1993, a young African American with two small boys was in the audience. During the Q&A period, he asked, "Do you have any idea how many young African American men die a day? Why do you make such a big deal about one death?" His eyes were ablaze with anger. My legs went weak, with my head spinning; I was confronted with a totally unexpected question. I closed my eyes a second and then these words came out of my mouth:

> You know, I am a child of the Korean War. As a child, I stepped over dead bodies, some of them those of my friends. The first corpse sent an electric shock through my body but as I saw more corpses, I became numb—no feelings.

> Day in and day out, people watch dead bodies on the tube and think nothing of it; people see too many of them too often. I wanted to humanize victims of that riot, dead as well as living. I wanted people to know that the dead body was young and alive before turning into a corpse and that he has a mother who will carry him in her chest as long as she lives. It is not that one death I am glorifying. I am saying that for each dead body, life was lost and there is a mother mourning.

Remember Rilke's prayer,

> Oh, Lord, give each of us his own death,
> The Dying, that issues forth out of the life
> In which he had love, meaning and despair.

And, in return, my own thoughts about how to find meaning from despair:

> *Go to the edge of the cliff by the sea.*
> *The waves are hitting the rocks.*
> *Listen to the whispers of*
> *The water.*

When misfortune strikes,
Look at new leaves,
Tender and green,
Sprouting on branches of trees.
See a ray from the brilliant sun.

When misfortune strikes
Run through the apple trees
Under a hot August sun
And delight in the shiny red apples,
The orchard before harvest.

Listen to the murmurs of your heart.
It is a treasure box of memories
Each wrapped in love.
              ~ dskg

I read a book, *Epilogue,* a memoir by Anne Roiphe, an author of 17 books and a widow who lost her husband to a heart attack. It is a *New York Times* bestseller. My friends Ilyon and her husband Joon ordered it for me.

As expected, her writing was good. She describes a widow's changed life skillfully and sometimes artfully—in fog, in confusion, in anger, in loneliness, in sadness, etc.

What struck me most was her certainty about the state of afterlife—NOTHING. She writes, "If I remember something about him, the Irish cap he wore, the time we drank ice-cold root beer at a road stand in Vermont, that is my memory sending neurons scattering about my brain. It is not his memory, which has disappeared into protein and atom, molecule and dust. Freudians do not believe in life after death, and neither do their spouses."

Her belief in NOTHING after death, she admits, deprives her of certain "easy comforts." "No meeting again in some heavenly place, no holding hands on a cloud, no merging of body and soul. Not ever again," she writes.

To her, death is an unending absence. So she envies "those who believe in a world to come. I envy those who believe that justice will come in the afterlife. I know that most of the world believes in some version of this story."

She accepts the death of her husband calmly and courageously. "But H is altogether gone. He is not in heaven. He is not in hell. He is not waiting for his bones to come together and rise again from the valleys of Jerusalem. I think this now without pain. I think this the way one notices that it is raining outside and an umbrella will be necessary. I have developed a thick skin, or at least a usable scab. Or am I bluffing?"

I respect anyone's views about the state of life after death. Certainly "Nothing" is a viable choice just like any other beliefs one chooses. From time to time, I get caught by that idea.

Then, why do I feel resentful or even offended by her? I detect a certain dismissive voice about all other beliefs about death as sentimentalities and melodrama. As I did often while Don was alive, I am taking her comments personally. I can just see this woman dismissing my feelings.

Her phrase, "certain easy comforts" gets under my skin. I hear myself saying, "Lady, there are no *easy* comforts when it comes to the loss of one's loved one, provided the love was real. It is not any more courageous or difficult to believe death as 'an unending absence' than as entering into heavenly glory. After all, the immediate pain comes from the absence of the physical presence, does it not?"

In comparison, I found what Mark Twain has to say about death and immortality in his autobiography extremely intriguing.

Whatever he wrote in that book, he is supposed to be saying from his grave, since he instructed that it could only be published after his death.

> When we believe in immortality we have a reason for it. Not a reason founded upon information, or even plausibilities, for we haven't any. Our reason for choosing to believe in this dream is that we desire immortality, for some reason or other, I don't know what. But I have no such desire. I have sampled this life and it is sufficient. ... Annihilation has no terrors for me, because I have already tried it before I was born—a hundred million years—and I have suffered more in an hour, in this life, than I remember to have suffered in the whole hundred million years put together.

He writes of death: "It is understandable that when I speak from the grave it is not a spirit that is speaking; it is nothing; it is an emptiness; it is a vacancy; it is a something that has neither feeling nor consciousness."

Clearly, his views about the state of life after death and the denial of immortality are not different from those of Ms. Roiphe. But Mark Twain does not get under my skin. Why? He is humble enough to say that no one really knows for certain about immortality whereas Ms. Roiphe is so *certain*—she knows; it is nonsense.

What touches me and even puzzles me about Mark Twain is what he wrote after he lost his wife, whom he calls his life, his beloved daughter, Susy, and his dearest friend, Mr. Rogers. He asks if he would bring the dead back if he could.

> Would I bring her back to life if I could do it? I would not. If a word would do it, I would beg for strength; I am sure of it. In her loss, I am almost bankrupt, and my life is bitterness, but I am content; for she has been enriched with the most precious of all gifts—that gift which makes all other gifts mean and poor—death. I have never wanted

any released friend of mine restored to life since I reached manhood. I felt in this way when Susy passed away, and later my wife, and later Mr. Rogers. When Clara [one of his three daughters] met me at the station in New York and told me Mr. Rogers had died suddenly that morning, my thought was, 'Oh, favorite of fortune to his latest moment!' The reporters said there were tears of sorrow in my eyes. True—but they were for me, not for him. He had suffered no loss. All the fortunes he had ever made before were poverty compared with this one.

I have one essential question: Could it be true that death is the most precious gift to the one who died? I wish Don would tell me if this is true. Part of me understands that whatever caused the death, the one who died was liberated from that cause, i.e., suffering.

If Don welcomed death as a gift more precious than anything he had in life and if he is in peace, I will learn more and more that my grief and pain are for me, not for him.

A disturbed dream last night.

> *I am in the Abbey of Gethsemani in Louisville, Kentucky, a monastery in the Order of the Cistercians of the Strict Observance. I see Trappist monks disappearing one by one.*
>
> *A thought crosses my mind, "They must be scattering to find penetrating, intense solitude in the silence of nature."*
>
> *Suddenly, I am startled to see the back of a monk slowly walking toward the path of creek gravel, then down the hill and across the fields. Far away in the field, he becomes almost invisible, small, like a little speck. But I know he is there and that he is my Don. "I found him!" Aghast and my soul stirred, I can hardly contain myself. I run to catch him.*

A shrill sound of phone awakes me. I reach the phone and just hang up. Whoever it is, I can't talk. I can't deal with it. Now fully awake and in sorrow of losing such a vivid dream with Don, I find a book to read.

Richard Feynman, a theoretical physicist, wrote, "You investigate for truth, because it is unknown, not because you know the answer." He insists that attitude of uncertainty should become a habit of thought, and that unknown must be recognized as being unknown in order to be explored.

He called it the "humility of the intellect."

Feynman further expounds how all life is interconnected with all other life. "So close is life to life. The universality of the deep chemistry of things is indeed a fantastic and beautiful thing." Amazingly, he wrote that "It is one of the most remarkable things that in all of the biological sciences there is no clue as to the necessity of death." Nothing in biology yet found indicates the inevitability of death.

So where do I stand this morning with all these—uncertainty, interconnectedness of all things, no indication about the inevitability of death, etc.

For today, all I know: Don was not annihilated. I know and believe this, not with dogmatic certainty but with loving uncertainty.

I blamed death for separating
Don and me.
For sure, death was the bridge
Don crossed

But we were never separated
The bridge never separated us
Don and I cross it all the time
Not on our feet
But in love

~ dskg

A YEAR AGO TODAY, DON HAD TO LEAVE this earthly life. It is like a dream—how I spent 365 days without him.

That unassuming, shy, intelligent and loyal man, Eugene Kim, wrote me:

Just letting you know, although I'd like to think you know already, that we're all thinking of you and of Don on this somber anniversary.

Has it really been a year? That's what the calendar tells me. But Don's presence was/is so vivid, the passage of time seems somehow irrelevant. He loomed large in life, and will continue to do so in our memories.

I find myself wondering what Don would have made of the events of the past year; I wish I could ask his opinion of how President Obama is doing. (I wish I could ask his opinion on a lot of things.)

American writer Damon Runyon once said, "You can keep the things of bronze and stone, and give me one man to remember me just once a year."

Today I found Don's writing about what he called "Near Death."

1. Automobile accident in 1957. I hit another car broadside and rolled the car end over end.

2. Summer of 1958, I fell asleep while operating a road construction implement and went down a thirty foot embankment barely missing a much deeper crevice.

This means he could have died in 1957 or 1958. Then I would have never even met him. I would have never known that the person by the name of Don Gibson existed! Put into this perspective, should I not be grateful that he lived to meet me and we lived together as husband and wife for 29 years?

Or should I not accept what Wordsworth wrote?

We die, my Friend,
Nor we alone, but that which each man loved
And prized in his peculiar nook of earth
Dies with him or is changed, and very soon
Even of the good is no memorial left.

O Sir, the good die first,
And they whose hearts are dry as summer dust
Burn to the socket.

Well, I can concede that the good die first but I hope my heart is not as dry as summer dust.

Just finished a book, *How We Die,* by Sherwin B. Nuland, a surgeon. I picked the book up when I was in Vermont at a used book store. The book's subtitle is *Reflections on Life's Final Chapter* but it is more technical and medical about various diseases than I had anticipated. I learned quite a bit.

I have long suffered about my medical ignorance. I often thought that I could have helped prolong Don's life if I knew more about his sickness. But Dr. Nuland writes about how his 62 year old brother died of cancer and how all of his knowledge and experience didn't help his beloved brother. At the end of the book, one memorable line: "When we mourn, it should be the loss of love that makes us grieve, not the guilt that we did something wrong."

He says nothing new but much of life is hearing the same message at a different time, with a different frame of mind.

He left me a widow
Like a hot-air-balloon
With a gaping hole.

He left me a widow
To cry alone
In the splendor of
The autumnal color.

He left me a widow
To putter alone
Looking for his traces
Only to feel the agony of betrayal.

He left me a widow
To weep like the Hebrews
By the waters of Babylon.

He left me a widow
With all the windows open
For him to fly in
To bring
An invisible presence
Dancing in the flooding sunlight.

~ dskg

TODAY I HAD A RARE PLEASURE of having dinner with our next-door neighbor in Chevy Chase, D.C. Our very first house. They were a young couple, African American husband and Caucasian wife, both lawyers, Chewani and Candice.

Since we moved away, we had learned that Chewani died of liver cancer. I recall how sad Don was at the news. Over a glass of wine, Candice told me about trials and difficulties of her life with two daughters. Chewani died at age 57. Candice was still young. I sensed that she was ready for a new life. I hoped that will come true.

Back home, I think of Don's death and my death. His is harder to take than mine, not because I don't really accept mine. I know I will die and if that's the end of everything and that there is nothing more, just the end, with my body turned into ashes, I won't even know that I am dead. My life that came around and stayed for a while on this earth extinguished. If there is more to death than nothing, I am with him. So I can take my death.

But his death? It still puts me in deep grief.

One of the most frequently repeated pieces of advice to me from friends and relatives is to "live life to the fullest." Underlying this is that grief prevents one from living life fully. I must disagree with this. If we mean by "living fully" that we live with a good grasp of what life is, grief certainly makes one's life fuller.

I am learning a lot about grief these days, grief as a companion of joy and compassion. While I learn about grief, I do not sit around. I write, paint, read and do a few things that might benefit others around me and those who are in need.

Maybe, I should organize a community of grief. Upon the second thought, I realize that human life should naturally be a community of grief since life is so full of suffering and that anyone with compassion should grieve with the fellow sufferers.

There are so many wars raging around the world. If the wars are not fought on the battlefields with a license for mass killing, small and large wars happen every minute on a daily basis at home, on streets and everywhere. With this, how can we not grieve?

But grief is lonely, because for the majority, sorrow is an unwelcome companion. Anyone who willingly enters into the pain of a stranger is a remarkable person. And there are only a handful of them. I am fortunate I have a couple of those friends. Don helps me most. Whenever I feel unbearable grief, I think of Don who was full of kindness and indomitable will, and his eyes to me, always full of love and sadness.

Have you ever walked on the streets of
A war-torn city?
I did, a fifteen year old girl
In my city of Seoul

The streets were covered with fog
Silent eloquence everywhere
Shadows of death
So many of them
Sons and daughters, brothers and sisters
Friends, young and old, male and female
That silence more piercing than
Howling animals

Neither the raindrops
Nor a thundering downpour
Can cleanse the dark blood
But the same humans
Continue to run wild. Blood thirsty
Murdering each other in the name
Of war.

~ dskg

Hudson River on a snowy day

In a way, death is learning to get along with nature's timing. I can try to think that nature's timing was up for Don and he had to go. Somewhere Jung said that the birth of a human being is pregnant with meaning. Shouldn't death be likewise?

Accepting death and knowing its meaning is part of our life. He helped me to do that with my death but I am still struggling with his.

I think about what new life means to me. For me, it can mean only one thing—learning to live with Don in spirit. Learning to hear Don in his silent response.

Now is the time for me to learn to be spiritual, not religious— the world of spirit in which I can hear Don's voice in total silence.

Beneath those brows were
His eyes, clear and hazel green
That kindled love to me,
That sent winter to exile,
And brought forsythia.

With the lovely forsythia
Each branch
Brings a moment of joy
As if awakened
From a torment of bare winter.
Don delighted in forsythia
Calling it gaenari
Its Korean name

With gaenari
The torment of his absence
Turns into a moment of joy.

~ *dskg*

"Well, Don, if you are bored—*dead*—find a way to come back to life, to me!" I say aloud and look at Don's photo, leaning against the tree. I feel as if he is going to walk out of there and come to me.

OCTOBER 5, 1959, I WAS 20 YEARS OLD in South Korea. It was the day of the funeral. My parents managed to find mourning clothes for all eight children, white Korean outfits made of coarse cotton. All of us, eight grandchildren, followed our parents who walked right behind a small coffin that held my grandmother's body, now motionless and breathless. Others—relatives, friends and neighbors—followed. Some Koreans hire people to wail but there was no need for that. All of us, eight children and my parents, wailed with such sorrow that the sound seemed to be reaching the sky and covering it with dark clouds. The sound of sorrowful and soulful wailing never stopped until we climbed a small hill of a Catholic cemetery on the outskirts of Seoul.

As we buried our grandmother, we wept and wailed until our chests and hearts felt like they might give out, and the clouds in the sky turned dark and thick with our tears. It was a day of deep sorrow, each of us hanging onto private memories of this woman, our matriarch, more precious than anything in the world.

In silence, I vowed that someday I would move her to our family mountain in Kumdani in the north so that she could rest by the side of her husband, whose life had ended long before I was born. Her body lay in the South, her country still divided. I have no idea if I will live long enough to go to Kumdani with her.

But I visited her with Don in 1987. Together we built a stone wall to protect her resting place from rain and storm. And together, Don and I, bowed a deep bow, three times touching our foreheads to the ground.

Stepping stones across the water, Korea

Spring

Blessed are those who mourn, for they shall
be comforted.

Matthew 5:4

Spring

Maybe Spring is too brief
But long enough to unfreeze
The waters where we drink
New life.

Spring is
Covering the bare branches
With new leaves.

Sunrise lights all seasons
But after the winter of loss
Fidelity to new life
Is brightest in the Spring.

~ dskg

APRIL 12, 2009. Don is dead and it is Easter Sunday, the first Easter since Don left.

What does this mean? Is his spirit alive? Is he waiting for me to join him? If so, I wish he would send me a stronger signal so that I can believe it with all my heart and live for that day, with some joy in my heart.

I am reading a small book, *Stories of God* by Rainer Maria Rilke.

But what makes a dead person different from someone who becomes serious and goes into seclusion to quietly consider the answer to something that has tormented him for a long time? Maybe the dead are the people who had withdrawn from everything in order to reflect upon life.

Or is it the living who turn deaf ears when that knowledge is available all the time?

April 4, 2010. The second Easter since Don left. I went to the roof of our building where the sweeping view of the Hudson River and Palisade Park sat in glory. I tried to feel Don floating up there but most closely in my heart.

What does Easter mean? For now, I know this: Don is not dead to me; he is alive with me.

That is Easter to me.

April 25, 2011. The third Easter since Don left me. Today I am desperate to find Don. After all, today is the day of resurrection. I do feel an unbreakable connection with him. Invisible, untouchable and inaudible as he is, I know he is alive, in a different form, or even in no form, but he is alive.

On this special day, I am further thinking that we not shy away from grief, be it mine or other's—love is the only force that will make us understand and practice human solidarity in death and suffering. If you grieve for what you love, you can't be indifferent to the sufferings of others, for you will have true compassion. Compassion that means "to suffer with."

I watched *On Golden Pond* in the evening. The play made into a movie in 1981, written by Earnest Thompson. It was the first play Don and I saw together at the Kennedy Center in 1979. Thirty-one years later, I watch the movie version alone.

Don and I didn't have a golden pond in the foot hills of New Hampshire's White Mountains by Squam Lake, but we did have the Hudson River and glorious sunset which we admired in unison every evening. I should remember that we did have our golden pond, our very own Hudson River. Besides, now I can go to all those places where we wanted to go without worries about Don's shortness of breath. I know he accompanies me everywhere I go.

The exquisite camera work of Billy Williams made me remember how Don was the only one who could take decent photos of me. There is no secret in that. It was his affection and his beholding of me as a beautiful woman.

This afternoon, I went to the Strand Book Store, Don's kind of book store. I saw Don everywhere in that store. He never made it to that store since when we moved to Manhattan in 2002 he was already short of breath from severe emphysema.

I went to that store to look for books by Howard Frank Mosher. They had two books by him, *On Kingdom Mountain* and *The Fall of the Year*. I still prefer browsing around the books in the store with their smell. I am yet to develop the joy of internet shopping.

Last night I talked with Don's old friend, Jerry Kelley, current mayor of Indianola, about establishing scholarship funds for students from the graduating class at Indianola High School in Don's memory. The high school where he taught in the early sixties and later wished that he had stayed.

I discovered Jerry in Don's writing. He spoke of Jerry fondly and regretted his failure to stay in touch. Apparently Don and Jerry were involved in political campaigns together. I was thrilled to find Jerry, an ideal person to help me with Don's scholarship. He agreed to work with me.

I know Don led me to Jerry.

EVENING. THAT GLORIOUS PINK FROM THE SUNSET is spread in the sky. A thought comes to me that in his death Don is managing (helping) me to be a writer.

I read *Letters to a Young Poet* by Rainer Maria Rilke twice on a recent Sunday, in which he writes much about solitude both as a gift and burden.

Rilke writes about solitude in relation to creativity. How "creativity" is inevitably linked to solitude because to create, one needs to look inside. He writes, "Find out the reason that commands you to write; see whether it has spread its roots into the very depths of your heart; confess to yourself whether you would die if you were forbidden to write."

For a long time, I've had a wish to become a writer but while Don was alive I honestly don't think I felt "I would die if I were forbidden to write." Well, after he died, I know I would have died if I were forbidden to write. Writing became what Rilke calls "necessity," if I were to go on living. Writing was the essential means to talk to Don and without that, I would not have lived.

Don at the peak of his career at NEH

Don was a brilliant manager and was always so good in delegating. But, as he wrote many times, he was not cut out to be a scholar or a writer. In order to do that, he needed patience and an ability to accept imperfection. He could deal with patience but not as well with imperfection. That's why he never completed his dissertation. He always completed management projects but was not very good in completing scholarly projects.

All this means that he was happy to stand behind and watch me shine. He did that with my filmmaking; and now in his death, he might be delegating me to finish up our joint memoir! When it is out to the world, he won't be under the limelight but will be smiling broadly behind me. I will make sure that people see him, whatever it takes.

My mind constantly goes to a fascinating turn of an event. Jim Leach, a long time Republican congressman from Iowa, an opponent of Ed Metzinsky (for whom Don was a campaign manager), and a recent convert to Obama, was nominated for the National Endowment for the Humanities chair. More fascinating is the fact that Don and Leach became good friends over the years, sprouting from the campaigning days in the 1970's. Don was sent by Metzinsky to debate Leach. The world surely goes around and comes around.

I think about how Don would have responded to Jim Leach's nomination.

I am up and sitting bewildered. I had a weird dream last night. Even more weird was the fact that I remembered the dream so clearly when I woke up.

> Don came to me and proposed "separation" for a while. I asked "why" for a separation and what he thought we could accomplish through this arrangement. He was silent. "If separation was the first step toward divorce, I would rather just get it done now," I said. Still silence.

> Some time passed and Don appeared again, this time in a suit and declared that he didn't want a separation. He wanted us to be together all the time. We hugged.

I woke up with that familiar touch.

So many people—friends, relatives, philosophers, theologians, poets and others—have told me that life is for the living and that I need to let Don go. He has his own journey to take. There are others who say that his soul can choose to fly far away but it can also wait around his loved one. I like to think that my dream tells me exactly that—that Don decided to wait and be with me.

When it comes to the matters related to death, no one owns the objective, factual truth. What I choose to believe is the truth for me.

I choose to believe that Don is close by me until we can fly away together.

Flowers will bloom again!
If I have to descend into the
Valley of thick fog
I will ascend into early morning mist
To be with you,
Through closed windows
Through open windows.

~ *dskg*

THIS MORNING I FOUND ON MY COMPUTER my application to the United Artists in 2008 for a grant of $50,000 one can apply for only if nominated. I still don't know who nominated me. I didn't get it but this was the last grant application Don edited for me.

Artists are a rare breed of people who live in agony and ecstasy striving to expand and transform human reality through their creative work. I may not yet be one of them but I work hard with a strong conviction that my films can transcend my abilities, if I let myself be guided by the voices and images of my subjects.

I focus on the oppressed, forgotten and neglected people with compelling and pressing issues. As narrators, they tell their stories to correct historical and political memories and inspire us to work with the present toward a better future. I would rather be a sympathetic listener with honest subjectivity than making human beings into issues, numbers and problems in the name of neutrality/objectivity. Ultimately we are all outsiders in the lives of others but I try to earn their trust and develop rapport with sensitivity, passion and devotion to truth.

If and when my film becomes art, it transforms into a human prayer, a plea and an attempt to redeem us, human beings.

I read an article in *The New Yorker*, The Good Cook (A Starving Patriot in North Korea). I wish I could talk about it with Don. I said many times to Don that if ever he recovered his health enough to travel, I would like to make a film about North Korea, perhaps my last documentary.

Right now, I am not sure if I can undertake such an enormous task in the absence of Don. Besides, I truly believe Don is now helping me to become a writer in his death as he supported my filmmaking.

This little article, however, inspires me somewhat. It is the first I ever read that invited the reader (viewer) into positive sides of ordinary citizens. So far the films made about North Korea are so obsessed about painting the monstrosity of its leader(s), Kim Il Sung and Kim Jong Il that all its citizens are presented as soulless dummies.

I always wanted to make a film about North Korea that humanized its citizens in the proper historical context. The United States, the country that proclaimed North Korea as one of the "three evils" of the world, was in fact deeply involved in keeping Korea divided until today. Were the US more sensitive to the needs of Koreans at the end of World War II, Korea could have remained a unified country under a unique socialist form of government.

This little article I read, based on one North Korean woman who ended up defecting to South Korea, takes readers to creative and resilient sides of the starved citizens, especially women, who cope with the hardest life ever imaginable. Their struggle is deeply inspiring. They should be inspiring to those who take every comfort in life for granted, like the majority of the US citizens, often including me. So my wish to do something about

North Korea is re-kindled, hopefully strong enough to keep it kindled until Don gives me a signal to move forward.

So here was a small spark of life by an article in *The New Yorker.*

TODAY I STRUGGLED ALL DAY to write about the impetus for establishing a Don Gibson Scholarship.

While searching for information that might help me on Don's computer, I found a couple of stories from Don's high school teaching.

1. I handed out the requisite evaluation forms of teaching performances. They were, as they generally are, quite positive because students understandably believe that a negative appraisal might be used against them. But I was particularly struck by one female student, who insisted upon signing her name despite the anonymity of the form. She planned to study medicine and was, apparently, brilliant in math and science but had great difficulty with the ambiguity of history. She wrote, "I hope Mr. Gibson is my patient sometime and I will cut his tubes." Indelicate but convincing.

2. At the end of the first semester, one year at Indianola High, the guidance counselor approached me and said that Tommy was flunking World History and that she had urged him to switch to a different course, one he could manage, for the next semester. As I taught it, World History was a tough course, virtually college preparatory, though not officially acknowledged as such. He insisted he didn't want to switch. "But why?" The counselor

*pleaded. "Well, Mr. Gibson is so excited about something
I just want to find out what it is." I raised his grade.*

Today, I HAVE A RUNNY NOSE, sore throat and coughing. But I
am working on our memoir. I remember how I used to yell for
Don's help every time I was unsure about spelling. I could have
looked up on the computer or in the dictionary but it gave me
an excuse to ask for Don's help, sitting in the room next to mine.
He never said, "Why don't you look it up?" He spelled it for me
without a word of complaint.

Now I'm mumbling, "Don, you are an asshole. You are delegating the task of completing the memoir to me. I can just hear
you say, 'Okay, you finish it up! I know you can do it! I am giving
that chance of completing our memoir with my death!'"

Well, that brings a smile to my face.

For several months, I tried to find Don's password for his
AOL account. Hawkeyes was the word Don used most often for
his password with different numbers attached. So I tried every
variation I could think of. I even tried to misspell that word.

This morning, I needed to explore his 2009 Day Minder. Oh,
my, my, I found two beautiful passwords on the first page of that
book. His AOL passwords for two different accounts. They were
there, all this time for me to find!

I am going to live, sending our password to him every day.

Today I finished reading, *Disappearances* by Howard Frank
Mosher, a Vermont writer we discovered together not long before Don disappeared. We come to this world and we all dis-
appear, one way or another, sooner or later. I witnessed Don

disappearing right in front of my eyes but I could not stop him.

Also today I am having extra trouble, darkened by profound skepticism about the value of our Memoir writing, especially mine. In desperation I wrote to our friend, Ileana, a brilliant philosopher/art critic in Houston. She wrote back.

Dai Sil:

This kind of doubt is universal. I always felt what I was writing was worth nothing and would not be read. Then I lost my inhibitions. It is not what you write but how you write it.

You cannot remain close to an absolutely 'realistic' narrative. It is only 'the other dimension,' that makes a narrative worth reading by others.

You are more than capable of transforming your most down-to-earth episodes into something that transcends both life and death.

It is very cold today but Kian, a four year old Korean boy, got me out of our apartment.

He asked his mother if he could have a Korean lesson today. I have no heart to say "No" to that little boy. So I had to go out to buy some cookies. He learned a wee bit but mostly we talked and he enjoyed his cookies and ice cream.

Lately, I have observed that I use the word "joy" reflexively, instead of "pleasure." I don't even have to think about it. I say "joy."

Co-incidentally, I find passage about joy in C.S. Lewis' book, *Surprised by Joy.*

There is an unsatisfied desire which is itself more desirable than any other satisfaction. I call it Joy, which is here a technical term and must be sharply distinguished both from Happiness and Pleasure. Joy (in my sense) has indeed one characteristic, and one only, in common with them; the fact that anyone who has experienced it will want it again.

I wish I could tell Don that now I am cancer free. I told my doctor that I was his "masterpiece." Slightly over five years since the doctor took out my entire stomach; now he declared me cancer free! I know Don was with me today as he had been with me when I was taken to that operation table!!

TODAY I SENT OUT LETTERS to the Don Gibson scholarship applicants. Only three will smile and all others will frown. Today was a day filled with meaning but also with profound sadness and loneliness. If only I could talk with Don about this scholarship. I think he will get a kick out of the fact that all three winners are female.

After I put the letters in the mail, I walked to Fort Tryon Park and sat on a bench with lots of sunshine.

TODAY I AM LOOKING AT ALL DON'S SHIRTS that I had ironed with such care—nice and smooth without wrinkles to hand them out one by one when he wanted to go out for walks and chat with his friends in our neighborhood coffee shops and bar.

Yes, he did look good despite his failing health and old age. Don was always a handsome man to me. Now I decided to wear those shirts myself as if I were walking with him.

Don reading, 2006

He looked very good in bright colors, especially in bright orange shirt which he wore to death. Alas, that shirt was burned in our house fire, and I wanted to replace it but nothing could be found like that bright orange. I did my best and bought a bright yellow and other colors combined. The shirt was too long. So I took it to the cleaners and shortened it. I believe he wore that shortened shirt once before he went away.

I see a small sail boat passing by through our window and I think of Don. He told me more than a few times that sailing was something he wanted to explore but we never did. We did, however, row a canoe on Saranac Lake a few times. He was very good with it and I was content to be with him on that canoe.

When I join him, perhaps the first thing we should do is to sail, not to fly. Flying will come in time. We will have eternity together and we will take our time doing things we have been unable to do.

The God I have been searching for all my life has always been within me, in the innermost depth of my being.

This makes me think what "reality" is. It is what one makes to be real. That is "reality." In the commonly accepted sense, the reality concerning Don, is "He is gone, dead." But in a way, I am constructing a new reality—the world in which he is gone but alive in my memory and love. So I am constructing a reality in which he is still living (June 25, 2010).

I went to a conference in Toronto organized for high school teachers to help them teach about the neglected aspects of World War II. I was one of the keynote speakers and was assigned to deal with the comfort women. The conference was organized by Chinese Canadians but there was a fair number of Korean Canadians who were involved. Most impressive among those at the conference was a large group of volunteers who took care of the guest speakers. They were polite, devoted young people. They touched me deeply.

My talk at the conference seemed to stir many hearts and minds. I shared with the audience my heart, full of grief and passion, and invited them to look back to the past that turned young women into sex slaves. While speaking, I thought I would explode with sorrow for those innocent lives that became such tragic victims of none other than fellow human beings. Oh, such unimaginable human cruelty.

Before coming home from Toronto, I spent a couple days with my niece, Mi Hee, her mother, David and Joshua. This is the family that took care of my mother during her final years on earth with three hot meals a day.

I visited my oldest brother, Daeil, at a nursing home. It was the same nursing home where he and other brothers thought of placing my mother, describing it as "an ideal place since there were other Koreans."

What I remember most are stories my grandmother told me many times about "brother #1." This was during the golden years before the division of Korea and the Korean War, etc.

When he was born it was the most joyous occasion of the Kim family. My maternal grandmother treated this baby as though he was more precious than a king. She told me many times how she tried to do everything for that baby boy, not to leave him in the care of our helpers. When he was old enough to urinate into the chamber pot, my grandmother personally held him to prevent his arse or anything else of his body touching the chamber pot. She was worried that it might be too cold for this precious baby.

I remember the time when my father and #1 brother announced that he was now a proud freshman at Yonsei University, one of the three best universities in Korea at the time. I also remember my brother wearing a baseball cap. Clearly my father wanted his #1 son to play baseball. My father was a baseball player at the university he attended in Japan.

The attention he received growing up with minute details always impressed me. Yet, I feared that he was not as strong or imaginative as my second brother (who vanished).

What I now feel for him is nothing but compassion for his life that is waiting to die in a nursing home far away from his land of birth.

Stepping inside the home to see my brother, I also remembered the day I spent with Don to see if indeed my mother could live there. Don and I agreed that we needed to examine the place before making a final decision.

At that time, I talked with an elderly Korean woman there in the rest home, a twenty-four-hour, bed-bound stroke victim. "How do you like this place? Is this better than being at home?" "Well, here at least I am not starving." "What do you mean?"

"Before coming here, I lived with my son. He and his wife both worked and were out all day. I was left alone with no one who could give me food. I was bed-bound and couldn't move around. Here they bring three meals a day. The food is absolutely tasteless but still it is food." "Are they attentive to your needs?" "Well, they bring me three diapers after the supper and leave them to me. I never understood how I would handle my own diapers." A long silence. "I am waiting for the day God calls me to him." I talked to a few other Koreans but the stories were all similar.

Don and I left the place with our hearts stricken with sadness and disappointment. We both determined that my mother could not survive the place more than a month. So we managed to have my mother live with Mi Hee's family. We did long distance supervision with as many visits as we could make from Washington, D.C.

It was in that very nursing home that my brother's wife and his children placed him, with what they thought were the first signs of Alzheimer's.

Now I am standing in the same building alone. My brother's eyes were at first blank when they saw me and then light returned to them slowly. "You are Dai Sil. Why is your hair so gray?" I tried a conversation but he only repeated he was waiting to die.

Suddenly, a long ago life in Pusan came alive in my memory.

It's during the war, 1951, I am 13; the city is Pusan, a port city, we are in two small rented rooms. The grandmother of our landlord made large quantities of kimchi to sell at a nearby market. Hence the house always reeked with the smell of garlic, ginger, scallions and red pepper, essential ingredients to be thrown into softened cabbages and turnips. If that kimchi smell wrinkled our noses, the stink coming from so many unwashed feet in one small house was almost unbearable. No, there wasn't much water to wash our feet, not to mention bathe.

Water shortage was a major problem in that crowded city, with refugees piled up.

Some of my siblings and I chose to spread a blanket on an open veranda close to the inner courtyard of the house for our bed instead of squeezing ourselves in a crowded room. One night, I was among those who wanted to sleep on the veranda. There was my brother #1 at the far side of the veranda, our maid, actually a rather delicate, beautiful girl who had been with the family many years, myself and one other brother. I don't remember which brother.

In that crowded veranda, with the war raging somewhere, we each dreamed of a different life. Perhaps we dreamed of love. My #1 brother rustled in the night, went to a spot which our maid occupied, stood there, and covered the sleeping maid with a small torn blanket. He then returned to sleep.

Now several decades later in a Canadian nursing home, I think of the war, the crowded veranda and my brother's eyes. Those were the dark days of the war, but our life was packed with future dreams.

I wondered what those eyes now saw. Whatever else those eyes saw, they saw my hair graying. Nothing glistens in his eyes now but old age and the dark shadow of death.

HOME AGAIN, IN THE MIDDLE OF THE NIGHT, unable to sleep, I read and found this in Kazantzakis' biography. "You want the simplicity that is found after complexity; not the other sort of simplicity that has not been contaminated by complexity." This is what I had in mind when I told Don that I wanted to die a simple woman. Don wrote that I was fooling myself. Well, he was right but now that he is gone, more than anything else, I do want this.

Don fits into Kazantzakis' description of "a tragic optimist." "A person who has confidence in man, who looks straight at the demon of destruction, hates it, but is not afraid of it, because he knows that all destruction is but the preparatory stage to new creation."

Don was entering the final phase of his life after he came back to Columbia Presbyterian Hospital on December 24, 2008, until January 3, 2010, if unconsciously. I remember one night finding him at 2 in the morning, going through his drawers, throwing things out with a full smile on his face. I was unable to sleep that night and came to my writing room. When I heard him in the next room, I asked if I could come, and heard his tender voice, "Of course." I found his face brimmed with peace. "Tonight I feel wonderful," he said. I could tell that at that moment he was free from pain. I rejoiced at that moment with him, never feeling anything but hope.

Although he was near death, that night I saw luminous joy in his eyes, the eyes good and mischievous, but also filled with so much sadness for such a long time.

"The soul has no limits," said Heraclitus.

TODAY I HAD VERIZON WIRELESS DISCONNECT DON'S CELL PHONE and made our family plan into a single one. More than a year and half since he went away. I have been charging his phone every night and put it on the computer desk and told him to call me if he needed me just like we did when he was around. Now that phone is disconnected. I feel so sad.

Yesterday, Candace Katz came to see us. I cooked her lunch and took her for a walk to Fort Tryon, ending up at New Leaf for coffee, a place Don loved, not for food but for its ambience.

Candace has a new book, a sequel to her mystery. I didn't open it while she was around but after putting her in a car, I came back to our apartment, sat down with a glass of wine and opened her book, *Schaeffer Brown's Detective Observations: Santa Fe.* There it was, her dedication.

For Donald Gibson, mentor and friend

I was moved beyond words.

I WAS WITH GRACE AND KEN IN ANNAPOLIS for a couple of days and now I am back with Don alone in our apartment. Grace gave me a book, *Anam Cara*, by John O'Donahue, that I started reading on the train coming back. I finished it this morning.

What touched me most came at the end, in his chapter about death. O'Donahue writes:

> Human experiences include all kinds of continuity and discontinuity, closeness and distance. In death, experience reaches the ultimate frontier. The deceased literally falls out of the visible world of form and presence. At birth, you appear out of nowhere, at death you disappear to nowhere. The absence of their life, the absence of their voice, face and presence become something that, as Sylvia Plath says, begins to grow beside you like a tree.

It warms my heart when he describes the Celtic tradition that the dead do not live far away. He further shows vividly that the Celtic Irish tradition recognizes that the eternal and transient worlds are woven in and through each other.

"Oh, my Anam Cara, my soul friend, I do feel our soul connection more and more each day."

A terrible dream lurched me awake.

It is twilight. The last ray of the sun lights the front yard. Don stands close to lilac bushes by the garage, smoking.

"Oh, here you are. I was looking for you."

"Now you found me."

"I wish I didn't find you smoking."

"Dai Sil, don't worry. Where I am now, smoking doesn't hurt me."

"Is that why you left me—to smoke freely?"

"Sometimes you can be so silly. No. I did not leave you in order to smoke."

"Then, tell me why you left me."

I thought a flicker of sadness passed through Don's face, contrary to what many said, that the dead do not have feelings, only the intellect.

"Dai Sil, please understand. I had to leave because death was the only cure for my ailing body."

Last night, I caught *Johnny Belinda* on TCM. Jane Wyman was superb. It is a tribute that she could not live with Reagan!

It was also shown on TCM while Don was alive. He came into our master bedroom, saw me immersed in that movie, my nose red and my eyes teary. He said, "Oh, Johnny Belinda! It's such an old movie. I saw it long time ago and liked it. Jane Wyman gave the performance of her life!" All the while I watched that movie last evening, I heard that voice.

Today I watched another movie, *The Heart is a Lonely Hunter.* The movie was made from a novel written by Carson McCullers, when she was only 23. I had seen it before on a big screen. All these years, the feelings from that movie had stayed with me.

Last year, I also picked up a copy of this book at the Strand Book Store, and read it. Alan Arkin plays the deaf mute and he was as good as I remembered him. An amazing performance—

to convey feelings of such tenderness, love, care, distress, grief, pain, and loneliness, without uttering a word.

Now I sit in front of my computer, still immersed in the feelings from *The Heart is a Lonely Hunter.*

I watched Obama for the longest time after Don left me. Don was so eager to witness him change America to be America again, but Don left three days before Obama's inauguration.

It was his second state of the union address. I listened to him. I would have loved to talk about it after the delivery with Don, but alone in bed, in deep thought, I tried to review my own feelings about Obama's speech.

The core of it was that America's standing in the world as the superpower of the world has been challenged and we must recover that. We must compete with China, Russia, India, etc., and win! We must remind ourselves of the meaning of "American dream" and renew that dream in every citizen. We must make sure that we are the #1 nation on earth.

In short, he went back to American imperialism and American superiority. He lamented foreign students and illegal immigrant students doing better than Americans!

"Don, forgive me but I feel disappointed. I hoped he would be more daring than becoming a practical politician with his second term in mind as soon as he crossed the threshold of the White House. I hoped that he would do and say things that would revolutionize and shake the world. I hoped that he would say that the world does not need superpower any more—we must learn to live together as equals.

"Am I a naïve dreamer? You were always a politician in the family. Do you approve of what Obama said last night?"

I am enjoying a piece of multigrain bread with raisins with

my freshly made French Roast coffee. At this moment, life is bearable. More than bearable. It is livable. I have to hang onto this moment and hope that it lasts.

Yesterday I had lunch with Susie Lim, a nice Korean-American woman, co-director of the Korean American Film Festival New York (KAFFNY). I enjoyed the lunch. I liked making Susie laugh.

Coming home alone, laughter was gone. Entering the apartment, I thought to myself, "If I can make Susie laugh, why can't I make myself laugh?"

Now I am reading *The Death of Adam* by Marilyn Robinson. She is a passionate defender of John Calvin. The book reminded me of my talks with Don about John Calvin and Martin Luther. Don was intrigued that I could remember the birth years of Martin Luther and John Calvin. I still do—1483 and 1509.

Robinson describes Luther, "brilliant, learned, coarse, robust, emotional." Don and Luther could have been twin brothers.

SIX YEARS AGO TODAY, my best friend Miae left us. Don was there when she closed her eyes and was carried out lifeless on a gurney by two white males.

What a sad day it was. I know Don was sadder that day than he had expressed. I read some of the things he wrote about that day. It has already been six years. Don lived four more years after she had departed from us.

Today I walked all the way to the Cloisters to pray for Miae's soul. I sat in the medieval church on a chair which I secretly designated as mine by the window, overlooking the Hudson River. I talked with Miae. The same chair I sat in and prayed for the recovery of Don's health.

I hope Don and Miae are together today.

My heart is filled with gratitude to Miae for her friendship and for her gift of painting. She had me paint in order to save herself from hearing endless stories of failed love affairs when I was a spinster. I remember the day when she made me stand in front of an empty canvas with some brushes and oil colors and ordered me to paint. When I protested that I could not paint, she said, "I know that! But try to occupy your head and heart to fill that canvas with something, anything, instead of telling me all those miserable stories about the failed love affairs!"

> *After a storm*
> *A morning calm—*
> *Cleansing and peaceful—*
> *Touches the wounded hearts.*
>
> *The moments of discontent*
> *Turn into joy everlasting*
> *As sweet as honey*
> *Savored by bitter mouths.*
>
> *After a storm*
> *A rough roar of water and wind*
> *Turns to quietude,*
> *Arriving in sunshine.*
> *As a simple act of mercy.*
>
> *~ dskg*

THE FIRST DAY OF 2010 IS HERE. I know one of the top priorities for Don during his last year on earth was to find a space where I could paint. He wanted me to resume my oil painting, which I had started in the 70's and stopped for a long while, strayed by my filmmaking and other sundries.

A terribly cold day. I am going to start painting today with Don in his room. I stand in front of my easel and look out of Don's window. My mind is blank. What to paint?

Then I see ice particles floating on the river.

That first winter (2002) after we moved into this place, Don and I looked out of the same window I am looking through now and exclaimed simultaneously, "Look at those ice pieces floating on the river!" "How beautiful!" We went on like that, as if a chorus.

Then I said, "Don, those ice pieces remind me of Monet's water lilies. So I am going to call them 'ice lilies.'"

We are getting the snow they had been predicting. Today, I would like to try to paint the snow covering the river. If I concentrate enough, I know I will catch the snowflakes falling on the river.

As I paint, I literally feel Don's hand with mine. He is holding the brush with me. So here I am living alone but painting with Don.

Today I went to 57th Street and Broadway to pick up some art supplies, specifically some brushes and missing colors. I had seven brushes and three colors picked out. When I was at the cashier to pay for them, I realized those brushes were more expensive than I had thought. I put three back. Still the total was over $100. The young man asked if I was an art student, and attended

Ice lilies on the Hudson

Iowa fields in winter

the school across the street. "If I were, do I get a discount?" "Yes," said he. "Then, I am." He burst into laughter and said, "No, I can't." I joined in his laughter.

Today I started my day right. I went right to my canvas and saw a shape emerging on the canvas and felt the joy of an amateur painter.

Lately, I have been thinking about what it means to be an amateur. I know that the dictionary links "amateur" to seeking pleasure rather than perfection or earning a living via vocation or job. I will be happy to remain an amateur painter. I want to be an amateur with joy in my heart.

TODAY I PUT A NEW CANVAS ON MY EASEL. I wanted to move from the Hudson River to an Iowa field, the winter, snow covered Iowa field.

A few times I was in Iowa with Don during the winter, I loved those fields—if desolate, it was elegant desolation; if it was icy cold, it was the cold beauty that can freeze one's soul into complete silence. It is the cold field that made a young boy's soul grow with dreams far beyond the misty horizon.

I made a broad outline of the field. All I could see was the field and sky in one. I could not tell where the field started and ended. It was linked to the sky.

I AM CONTEMPLATING A SERIES OF KOREAN BRIDGES. Life is full of bridges for us to cross, including the final bridge. I've always loved Korean bridges. They are so full of Korean emotion, fragile but resilient.

Bridges have lots of meaning these days, feeling as if I were standing on one of them, to cross to find Don. But I won't cross until I am done with a few tasks, God willing.

Korean bridge in winter

I have started two canvases on which I am putting down images of Korean bridges, one, a collection of small stones (it's on page 109), and a wooden bridge.

We went to York, Maine, and stayed at Cliff House at least once a year, preferably in late fall. Don and I loved sea roaring on before us, waves hitting the age old rocks, more magnificent than any sculpture pieces, and tiny flowers coming out of those rocks. We loved Maine. We continued going to Maine even after we moved to New Paltz, New York.

During one of those visits, we went out to our favorite lobster joint. He wore a white shirt with red suspenders. We sat by the window and I took a picture of him. That photo became one of my favorite ones. I based a portrait on that photo. As I painted on the canvas, he came alive for me.

That portrait is definitely my Don. It hangs on the kitchen wall. I can see it as I am sitting, or coming and going. As I eat alone, I always lift my wine glass toward that portrait and he never fails to grin back.

Well, the second Thanksgiving Day since Don's departure is over but I am trying to live with "thanks" in my heart every day. Nothing is better than "thanks" to fill one's heart.

Today I am going to work on Don sitting on a bench in the middle of a lawn with Iowa field at his back. I believe I took that photo the last time when we were in Iowa for his father's funeral.

I was thrilled to find a small Lutheran church on a hill while we were driving around. I loved that church and went inside and prayed for the recovery of Don's health.

Don sits on a bench, his hands folded and looking down, deep in thoughts. I title it in my heart, "A Philosopher."

I continue to work on Don's portrait sitting on a bench in front of that Lutheran church. He sits there, so immersed in thought, emotion and pain.

York, Maine, 2004

He was already very sick then and was suffering from a deep sense of inadequacy about himself, not contributing to society, pain added each day from his debilitating health. He was, perhaps, already wondering how many years, days were left for him on earth.

As he sat there, perhaps all his childhood memories were flooding back to him, with deep longing for his parents, both gone. How he had dreamed about seeing the world out there.

Now back old and frail, mourning his father's death. So much is embodied in that face and body.

I had an urge to meet Don when he was a boy.

I started Don's portrait from a photo of him at age 11. The cutest boy I ever saw. He wore a shirt with some kind of flower print and a sweater. Since the photo is a black and white, I can't tell the color of his clothes but I am sure they were well-matched. I am going to dress him as I like to. I am taking the liberty. The portrait of 11-year-old Don is on page 45.

I STARTED A NEW PAINTING, DON READING. No Don story would be complete without a book in his hands. I wonder if all that reading helps him where he is now.

For Don, the life of the mind was never a flight from reality but confronting it and making it better.

I am thinking about what my paintings are. They are copies of nature or photos, seen and copied with hands and minds that have no inborn talent. But they are mixed with most intense persistence and resilience, deepened with feelings that well up in me and saturate my body, mind and soul.

I declare each painting "quit" when I can no longer persist to whatever end I have been striving. So I do not know if my paintings can be categorized—impressionistic, realistic? If they are impressionistic, that's because I can't make them real. If they look somewhere between "realistic" and "impressionistic," that's because I can't be either.

I wish I could paint from my memories alone but I can't. I have to use photos, but no portrait of Don is just a copy. I put

Don, a philosopher, Iowa 2006

Don in Scotland, 1994

my memories, love and soul into them. Every time I finish a painting, I feel like shouting, "Don, what do you think? Do you like it?"

But today I think of the time Miae went to Korea, sat in a cold room and copied the entire Bible from the beginning to the end, countless times, while waiting for her run-away husband to return.

I SPENT THE ENTIRE DAY ORGANIZING MY COMPUTER FILES with some help from a beautiful Korean woman (Anna) who is an interior designer but also good with the computer.

My files were such a mess. I had a fear that the computer would rebel and just crash on me, but today Anna helped to put everything in order. I feel so good about it. I know Don is proud of me. I find myself talking to Don. "You always told me how you didn't understand my files. Well, now it's time for you to come back and check them out, asshole."

Among the things she did was to take pictures of some of my paintings and put them in the computer.

I received quite a few responses from friends.

Carolynn Reid-Wallace wrote, a long time friend of Don and me who lived in Chevy Chase, D.C., where our first house was. She is an African American woman of vision and talent. Her last position was President of Fisk University.

> I just printed off those remarkable paintings that you shared with me. I truly believe that you missed your calling. You capture fully the essence of Don—the mischievous grin, the haunting, faraway look that sometimes

came into his eyes, the former man of youth still beaming out from a face that had seen the heights of joy and
depths of despair. That, my friend, is a gift.

Yet another response from Martin Everett, one of Don's
neighborhood friends.

> I am not used to anyone knocking my socks off at
> OH-dark-thirty in the morning. Dai Sil, your paint-
> ings are wonderful. When I saw the first one of Don,
> my mouth dropped open to my chin, what a wonderful
> depiction of the essence of the man. WOW! You capture
> such serenity in your paintings, you can feel the breezes,
> bask in the sunlight and smell the freshness of the fertile
> earth. Oh to be in Iowa and N. Korea.

Charles Burnett, much respected and loved film director/
writer and a friend.

> You captured Don's expression. The longer you look
> at his paintings, the more he comes alive. It is the angle
> and a combination of his smile and eyes that compel you
> to stare back. I ask myself 'What is he thinking? What
> does he see that I don't?'

YESTERDAY, MARYANN TOOK ME TO SEE the movie, *Of Gods
and Men*. It was a French movie, directed by Xavier Beauvois. A
movie telling the real story about eight Trappist French monks
who lived in a monastery in Algeria with a poor community in
the 1990s.

I don't know when I was so deeply grabbed and touched by
a movie. The chants they sang were nothing other than heavenly voices and the face of each monk spoke so eloquently about

the state of his soul, in touch with or sometimes in conflict with God. There was a scene in which they sat, sharing a glass of wine and listened to Tchaikovsky's grand theme from *Swan Lake*. It will stay with me for the remaining days of my life.

When the captured monks walked through the snow, if only I could have as much faith as those monks!

LAST NIGHT A BROKEN DREAM. Suddenly I realize that Don and I are back to the Isle of Arran, Scotland. I was saying,

"We are back to Scotland together, your ancestral home."

"They went to Ireland in the eighteenth century, then from Ireland to America during the potato famine of the 1840s."

"Potato famine?" I find Don and me standing in a large vegetable garden where rows and rows of spring onions and garlic grow.

"Where are we?"

"Dai Sil, it's a vegetable garden at the back of your childhood home in North Korea.

"How did we get here?"

Don tells me to dig potatoes. As my hands dig into black soil, I let Don's hand go. I feel startled.

Now Don stands apart from me.

"Dai Sil, I have to be on my way now. You must go back with these potatoes to feed the children of the world."

There was a time in my youth
When I wanted to wear a silk dress
Looking soft and elegant
Dreaming of my soul mate.

Now my hair is gray
A nose where deep sorrow flows
Eyes watery with longing
Now my soul mate has lived and gone.
I would rather wear a coarse cotton dress
Looking for a patch of blue in the sky
Dark with clouds.

I want to walk on the scarred earth

To look for starving children in abandonment
My chest heaving with hope
To give them a moment of fullness.

~ dskg

YESTERDAY I DID TWO THINGS THAT STAND OUT. I woke up at 6 am, worked until 12 and then ventured out. I wanted to catch a special Korean exhibition at the Metropolitan Museum, which was supposed to blend modern abstract paintings and traditional Korean art work, especially ceramics.

So I rode the M4 bus for an hour to get there. I read *On God: an Uncommon Conversation*, by Norman Mailer with Michael Lennon.

The Korean show was somewhat disappointing. It had only two paintings by a New York-based Korean American artist, Il Lee, born in 1952. Such a young artist to have his paintings exhibited at the MET. I thought of Miae and her lost opportunity as a painter.

What was more meaningful for me was to see paintings by Van Gogh and Cezanne since I am into their work with my recent portrait paintings of Don.

I was so exhausted that I could hardly sit through the bus ride home. At some point, I was afraid I might collapse in the bus. Back home, I checked my emails briefly, heated up some corned beef that I had cooked and ate with a glass of red wine.

The more major event was at 8 pm on TV. Turner Classic Movies played *East of Eden*, John Steinbeck's work, with James Dean and Julie Harris. James Dean was a genius, such a natural born, brilliant actor. How his character in the movie was broken when his father refused to receive his money and how the movie ended with his redemption—his father with a severe stroke, paralyzed and lying down, whispering to his son, "Don't get any one to help me. You stay and take care of me." And the love-starved son, pulling his chair to sit by his father.

Grace and her husband Ken are reading our Memoirs that are in progress. She wrote me today:

> The more I read the larger than life he becomes. This
> is a true American hero. This is America in personifica-
> tion and the book evokes his spirit. You have a winner
> in this book. I know one when I see one. The question
> is how much do we benefit in soul work and how much
> does the world reward that—always a mismatch.

She wrote that the experience of reading our manuscript "has acquainted me with the meaning of love in a face never seen before." She said our memoir is "heart going before the word."

This weekend, the Korean American Film Festival in New York is presenting a retrospective of my films, six of them: *A Forgotten People, Motherland, Sa-I-Gu (April 29), Wet Sand, Olivia's Story,* and *Silence Broken.*

MARCH 19, 2011. WE SHOWED FIVE FILMS TODAY. From our neighborhood group, Daniel and Harold showed up.

It wasn't the best attended screening, especially the 2 pm one, but *A Forgotten People* was beautiful. *Motherland* was okay, too. The discussion afterward was fun. Ewha Girls' High School graduates (my *alma mater*) brought a bouquet of flowers for the screening. I put those flowers by our urn where Don rests now.

The 5 to 8 pm program that included the screening of *Sa-I-Gu (April 29), Wet Sand,* and *Olivia's Story,* went well. It was a well-attended screening but the highlight of the program was the discussion afterwards with Mrs. Lee, and Charles Burnett.

Mrs. Lee lost her only son during the 1992 riots and she is in both of my LA riot films. All these years, all of the screenings and festivals invited scholars and leaders to tell how she must have felt and why. This was the first time that I was able to persuade festival directors to invite Mrs. Lee. Charles Burnett is an African American director/writer who worked with me all these years, a colleague, friend and mentor in filmmaking.

It was quite an experience to translate Mrs. Lee's sorrowful and moving talk, and listen to Charles. He relayed his stories about living in South Central, as a boy, among other views.

South Central borders the Westside on the northwest and Downtown Los Angeles on the northeast; it refers to a large geographic and cultural section where primarily African Americans lived. For the past couple decades, more than half of its population consisted of Latinos. In 2003, the City of Los Angeles changed the name to South Los Angeles in an attempt to disassociate it from urban decay and street crimes. But it is still largely known as South Central.

I had not seen them for a long time. I found all three films strong and moving. I was glad that I made them but without Don they could not have been made. In every film I made, his name is at the top of the special "thanks" list.

The Forgotten People made me think of him so much—all those faxes he sent while I was on that island for a month! I still have them.

Don had given me blessings to travel to this frozen island to make a film about forced Korean laborers. North of Japan and a few miles off the Eastern Coast of Siberia, the island has, for centuries, been a disputed territory between the Japanese and Russians. At the end of the Russo-Japanese War, the island was divided and the south became a Japanese territory, called Kara-futo. It was to Karafuto that tens of thousands Koreans were brought by Japan in the early 1940s to exploit rich natural re-sources for the imperial war efforts.

It was a packed day and I was exhausted. All day long my heart was filled with gratitude and longing for Don. But I was careful not to indulge too much in my own pain when I had a mother who lost her only son, a month before his 19th birthday.

Harold, an African American historian, a good friend of Don's with whom Don had numerous conversations, especially on historical topics, was at the screening for *Sa-I-Gu*, *Wet Sand* and *Olivia's Story*. Los Angeles is Harold's home territory.

Dear Dai Sil,

I was dumb struck by your two films on the LA Riot. They were the best things I had seen on civil unrest in America, particularly my own city, ever. I missed these films when they were shown on PBS. They need to be preserved as perhaps the most important near contemporary accounts of these central, though tragic, events.

As blacks, Latinos, Koreans, Chinese, American Indians, and whites reel from the rapid changes in American and world affairs, we need documentarians to record and analyze the world as it emerges from its infancy into a new adulthood. I hope you have the energy to continue to create in film and other media, and also teach and encourage younger generations to see the world clearly and make lives in politically relevant arts.

Today I did something out of my routine life. I met old friends Nancy, Andrea and Abbie, for a play and dinner afterwards. We went to see *A View from the Bridge*, the most recent revival of a 1955 play by Arthur Miller. Gregory Mosher directed it and the stars were Liev Schreiber, Scarlett Johansson and Jessica Hecht.

As I climbed the stairs in Cort Theater to the balcony, I thought of Don. He could have never made it up to the seats. All our dreams of catching the plays and museum shows in our retirement never came true. When we moved to northern Manhattan, Don was already too sick to negotiate steep stairs in the theaters and subways, or stand in long lines to buy the last-minute tickets.

If we saw *A View from the Bridge* together, we would have had a lively discussion, especially about the on-going issues of immigration and illegal immigrants.

America is a nation of immigrants. Everyone in this country is an immigrant or child of immigrants, except for Native Americans. Yet those who seized the power early on, and wrote a constitution of liberty and inalienable rights, are treating "immigrants" as if they are robbing the country. This and other social issues were our on-going discussions.

Listen to me, America
Where pilgrims landed
And built the nation
With slave labor
From the continent of Africa

Don't you remember
When we were all nomads
Traveling the universe
Across the uncharted seas and lands?

Why not welcome other nomads to join
Who come saturated in sweat and sorrow
Through the thunder and storm

~ _dskg_

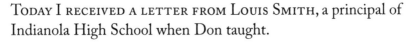

TODAY I RECEIVED A LETTER FROM LOUIS SMITH, a principal of Indianola High School when Don taught.

After all these years, Mr. Louis Smith is still alive. I am glad he is going to come to the first Don Gibson Scholarship Award ceremony and say a few words. He wrote:

He [Don] was one of the finest teachers I have ever known. When he and another outstanding teacher (of French) were both on the faculty, over half of the students in the high school were enrolled in either German or French classes, unheard of in a small town, semi-rural setting. His classes were always filled to capacity. I might add that many of his students have gone on to substantial careers to what I would credit as his influence.

The fondest recollection I have of anything about him was one day when the school librarian came to me with a several-weeks-old paycheck belonging to Don. Don had been using that as a bookmark. I sought Don out to return the check to him, and he had forgotten all about it. This was classic Don Gibson.

A NIGHT NOW AT PUTNEY, VERMONT. The Woos invited me to their family house deep in Putney Mountains, a house designed by Mr. Woo, an architect, for the generations of Woo families to come and share their lives.

An incredibly beautiful night in an elegant house in the mountains. No outside intrusion. Just the family and friends with whom they want to share the space.

I am in their guest room in total silence. A dark night. Without looking out, I can see the stars in the sky through my mind's eye. Cold, shiny stars strewn in the night sky.

I woke up to a Putney morning in which a magnificent house was fully revealed in sunlight. It is thoroughly modern but unassuming, with huge windows that bring inside the outdoors. A perfect marriage, bringing nature inside.

I sat with Mr. and Mrs. Woo and had a cereal breakfast. They took me for a walk. I guess we walked about two miles. So many white birches and pine trees brought Don to me. He loved those trees. We admired white birches in New England and pine trees in Korea.

I am a wanderer in my heart
As long as I breathe
I will fly with shifting winds
To look for summer storms
Which my soul mate loved

I will raise my eyes to mountains
Walk through thick forests
Let my eyes lead me to a remote village
Where candle light burns in the houses.
Where whispers are elevated to love.

And I will not forget to smile
At the first dawn
Which I know will recur.

~   *dskg*

This morning, while working on our memoir, I found Don's writings about his trip to Iowa in 2003, which he took alone, when I went to Pusan International Film Festival.

He wrote how he felt about his father wanting him to buy liquor. At first, he was a bit concerned. Then he changed his mind.

Upon further reflection, I see nothing, absolutely nothing wrong with my Dad's wanting to drink. He is dying; he wants to die and die soon. He's in pain. I don't know how much of it is physical, but for sure emotional pain is real. Let him find comfort where he can. Almost every time I call he expresses despair about how he should have led a better life, been a better father. He is wrong, but I fear his expressions are sincere.

This made me think of Don who so much identified himself with his father. And I identified with Don and his feelings about his father when he wanted to have gin and tonic in the afternoon.

Don was not supposed to have hard liquor and, for that reason, we didn't keep hard liquor at home. But one day while buying a case of red wine, I saw Bombay Gin in a beautiful bottle. I had always loved that gin bottle more than its content. I could not help it. I bought one and Don's eyes, which missed nothing, saw that bottle.

In the afternoons, he said, "Dai Sil, it is time for a little gin!" with the voice that carried delight and excitement. At first I was terribly concerned and felt guilty. Then I changed my mind. I thought about his pain and how he was deprived of so much in life. If a little gin helps him, why not? I still remember his face when I brought him a little gin in the afternoon.

It is unbelievable that I fly to Indianola, Iowa, tomorrow morning to award the first year Don Gibson scholarship.

DURING HIS FINAL YEAR ON EARTH, Don and I talked about "leaving" in our lives. "Leaving" to find a new home was what we discussed. We never dared to talk about final leaving, both gripped by fear.

I found this on his computer:

There were many leavings, e.g., leaving the farm, leaving parents, leaving college, leaving high school teaching, leaving graduate school, leaving politics, leaving Iowa, leaving Washington, D.C., leaving work.

Yes, indeed, there were many leavings. And most of those leavings were to seek something better. I also had many leavings in my life, the most fundamental being my first leaving—leaving my birth place in North Korea. I didn't exactly know then but now I know all my leavings were to find Don. Once I found him, I didn't leave. Why would I? I found my home. There was nothing better I would leave for.

One winter daybreak,
my grandmother pulled me
from the house in North Korea
hastening me to walk
with a knapsack on my back.

Stunned and frightened,
I asked "Where are we going?"
"To South Korea."
"What's in the south?" "Democracy."

"I don't want it. I want to stay here."
I was seven then.

After all these years
from across the ocean
that winter morning is never forgotten
But something miraculous happened.

I found my soul mate.
my home in life and in death.

~ *dskg*

Korean jars of soy bean sauce

Well, the first scholarships in memory and honor of Don were awarded on May 27, 2010, at Indianola High School.

Back to New York, I wrote to many of the attendees. Brenda, his former student and now the English teacher, wrote back.

I remember Mr. Gibson for his passion for history. He was so young and enthusiastic that he would literally jump around the front of the room while he was lecturing and writing notes on the board. He taught me how to write a great essay. He challenged me and we had many arguments because I was pretty much a straight A student, but I think he always gave me an A-. When I went to Simpson and took Western Civ it was the easiest A I ever got because he had me totally prepared.

When I became a teacher, I wanted to be a combination of three teachers that really affected my life and learning: he was one of them.

I REMEMBER THE TIME WHEN I TIP-TOED INTO DON'S ROOM while he was sleeping, sat silently in front of him and gazed at his face in repose. A few times as I tried to cover his bare feet, I unintentionally woke him up. He was startled, but seeing my face, he gave me the gentlest smile. At those moments, all I wished was to take away his pain. Now I go to his room and find the empty bed, just as I cleaned and remade it a few days after he went to the hospital that last time. I wanted the bed fresh and ready for him to come home and reclaim it.

Yesterday, I looked into a small bag in which I brought all the things Don had at the hospital. It took me a year and four months to open that bag. I could not bear to look at the contents.

The first item that drew my attention was a wrist watch Don loved. I had bought it at the Museum of Modern Art gift shop. He was visibly happy with it.

There was a time when that watch did not work and I saw Don distressed. I took it to a shop in Fort Lee. As I had suspected, the battery was dead. Don was so delighted to get his watch back. He wore that watch in the ICU. When it was taken off his wrist for some tests, etc., he was careful to keep it safe in his bedside drawer and made sure that I knew about it.

I sat with that watch for a long while.

I finally stood up, determined to have the watch cleaned up. I put a new battery in, and wear it feeling the pulse of his arm, the arm which wrapped around me so many times.

And to keep the time with him.

> *I hear Don's voice.*
> *"I am not lost*
> *You didn't lose me*
> *If darkness makes us invisible to the other*
> *Look for a glimmer of light*
> *To find a little boy in an attic*
> *With the orange of the fire in the stove*
> *If my absence makes you cry*
> *Look for the feet of a farm boy, wet by the dew*
> *The hands of a young boy, caked with earth,*
> *That black Iowa earth*
> *Harbor no sorrow for that boy*
> *The boy found a home with you*
> *In life and in death."*
>   *~ dskg*

I remember what he said on January 15, at the ICU of the Columbia Presbyterian Hospital three days prior to his final departure. "Dai Sil, Listen to me carefully. Because you don't listen carefully, you often misunderstand me."

Everything has changed for me since he left. Nothing is the same since he closed his eyes. Hazel green eyes, laughing eyes, eyes shiny with compassion, eyes that spoke love to me in silence.

Now I am learning to hear him in silence. Now Don is teaching me how to listen. I know it will take enormous patience. That's another thing—I was so impatient with him. I realize listening and patience are related.

Spring turns to Summer, then to Autumn, but I am ready. Memories return and take me to the reservoir of love where nothing is separated.

I hear the songs of crickets
In the summer night. I see
The narrow paths of rice paddies
Left behind, long ago, in Korea.
The moon makes green rice plants glow.
The song of crickets
Untangles my pain.
Green rice plants sway
Soon to become golden
To ripen in the autumn sun.

~ dskg

Iowa fields in Autumn

Dai Sil Kim-Gibson

Dai Sil Kim-Gibson is a North-Korea-born American. She is a renowned independent filmmaker/writer, known for championing the compelling but neglected issues of human rights. Her film credits include America Becoming, Sa-I-Gu, A Forgotten People: the Sakhalin Koreans, Wet Sand, Olivia's Story, Silence

Broken: Korean Comfort Women *and* Motherland (Cuba Korea USA). *All of her films have garnered national and international awards. They have been screened at numerous festivals worldwide, and have been broadcast nationally on PBS and on the Sundance Channel in the United States. Among other distinctive honors, she has received awards from the Rockefeller Foundation and the MacArthur Foundation. She also received the Kodak Filmmaker Award.*

She has served as Director of the Media Program at the New York State Council on the Arts; and as Senior Program Officer of the Media Program at the National Endowment for the Humanities. Formerly professor of Religion at Mount Holyoke College, she holds a PhD in Religion from Boston University.

An author of numerous articles, Silence Broken: Korean Comfort Women *was her first book (*The Philadelphia Inquirer: *"unforgettable.") She has completed a joint memoir,* Shoulder Friends, *with her late husband, Donald D. Gibson, formerly Acting Chairman of the National Endowment for the Humanities under President William Clinton.*